"*Revolutionary. Why? To* ... *e to tossing out learning. We spend a lot* ... *and growth. In* Assessment 3.0, *Mark Barnes focuses on the revelation and growth of the Independent Learners— our students. This is a great read for any teacher or administrator.*"

—Creed Anthony, Teacher/Writer of
"Your Parent-Teacher Conference" weekly column on LifeofDad.com

"*I loved every single concept, proposal, and piece of advice in Mark Barnes' latest book,* Assessment 3.0: Throw Out Your Grade Book and Inspire Learning. *Do you want a vision to revolutionize our relationships with students? Read the book. Do you want a blueprint for how you, as a teacher or administrator, can create a learning environment that nurtures high functioning citizens? Read the book. Do you want a class structured so that each child is academically challenged, and supported to meet challenges? Read the book. Barnes joins the ranks of educators, who through his words and actions, is saying, 'We are now the means of extraordinary changes in our schools.'*"

—Jeffrey Benson, Author, *Hanging In:*
Strategies for Teaching the Students Who Challenge Us Most

"*This text contains outstanding resources for communicating to stakeholders who care about how assessment systems can impact student behaviors and performances. If you are interested in changing how students and teachers view traditional grading systems, this book is a must read.* Assessment 3.0 *can be a revolutionary tool.*"

—D. Allan Bruner, National Board Certified Teacher

"*Mark Barnes is a leader and revolutionary voice in the movement to rid our educational system of an outdated assessment model. In* Assessment 3.0, *he delivers a persuasive pitch that current grading practices are both poor reflections of learning and damaging to students. Not only does he clearly define the problem, he offers a powerful solution with his SE2R model and delivers a blueprint for implementation that can transform classrooms and schools.*"

—Dave Burgess, Educator, Professional Development Speaker,
and Author of *Teach Like a Pirate*

"This book could turn the teaching community on its ear! A new way to assess students without letters or numbers—a novel approach to grades."

—Diane Callahan, Retired Teacher

"Nothing destroys a student's creativity and passion for learning as quickly or as completely as grades. Mark Barnes examines how that happens in Assessment 3.0, but he does much more than simply critique standard assessment tools, which have remained virtually unchanged in America for over 100 years. The veteran teacher guides readers through a fascinating investigation of how throwing out grades, while embracing digitally-enhanced independent learning, fosters a superior learning environment—one that also does a far better job of developing real-world skills that prepare students to excel in the world of tomorrow. This book has completely transformed how I approach teaching, and I can't recommend it highly enough to anybody interested in the future not just of education but also our nation."

—David Cutler, National Association of
Independent Schools Teacher of the Future

"Mark has done something important in writing this book. He argues—clearly and with hope—for specific, actionable change right now in our early 21st century classrooms. Here's the potential, here's the problem, and here's a way forward. This is a practical model for ed reform in general.

Assessment 3.0 illuminates the ample underbelly of traditional education practice by shining a floodlight on one of the most powerful icons—and relics—of its past: the letter grade. Rather than simply criticizing grades as "harmful," Mark presents a compelling case for the impact of grading practices on how students learn, and in doing so maintains focus on the reason we're all here—students and learning.

A recurring theme throughout the book is one of practice and application— honest assessment of what works, and ideas for making it happen. The book is, then, imminently useful for any educator— those wanting to think about their craft, and those simply looking for ideas for tomorrow morning. In that way, there can't be higher praise."

—Terry Heick, Director of TeachThought

"The way we assess student development and student work is a source of frustration to thousands of student, parents and teachers across America. With Assessment 3.0, Mark Barnes challenges us to rethink the traditional A–F grading scale in favor of a more results-oriented methodology of providing feedback to our students. Whether you abandon your gradebook completely after reading this book or merely turn a critical eye toward your practices as an educator, this book is an important and vital lens on thinking about teaching, learning and the role of assessment."

—Chris Lehmann, Founding Principal, Science Leadership Academy

"This book will convince any reluctant educator to rethink the traditional grading system. If Mark's vision can become a reality, students will be prepared for a world that doesn't reward A's and condemn F's."

—Angela Maiers, Educator, Author, Speaker and Founder of Choose2Matter

"As an educator working with the district office, I am given many different books to read throughout the school year. Some are rather dry and have too much technical information. This book was an easy, enjoyable read. The cases and "real world" aspect of the way the book was written made me want to try this form of grading in a classroom tomorrow. School districts across the country have turned to standards based instruction, standards based report cards and Assessment 3.0 is the next logical step to grading."

—Shelly Miedona, Math Coach

"Current achievement-driven, testing and grading-focused school cultures offer little insight into teaching and learning—often fostering negative self-esteem and pressure on students. Through logical argument, practical instructional moves, and a clear passion for children and their learning needs, Mark Barnes pushes our thinking and invites us to imagine a different path for education. I look forward to sharing Assessment 3.0 with colleagues. It promises to be a game-changer for schools."

—Donalyn Miller, Author of The Book Whisperer and Reading in the Wild

"Barnes is bold, insightful and right! It is time to not only throw out your grade books, but all the misinformation in your brains that supports the need for grades! None of us became teachers so we could have color-coded grade books. We became educators to make a difference in the minds of our students. This book shows us how!"

—Russell J. Quaglia, President/Founder

"*Quality feedback trumps numbers in nearly every scenario. A number or grade indicates the learning is complete. The use of SE2R allows educators to get to the heart of instruction . . . student learning. It provides a framework for a continuous discussion that is about learning, not an assigned number. Mark Barnes does a fantastic job of providing the research on the divisive nature of our current grading policies and offers an alternative that lends itself to student ownership of learning. I highly recommend this book to educators at all levels and in all content areas.*"

—Joe Sanfelippo, Co-Author of The Power of Branding: Telling Your School's Story

"*With a crisp, engaging style, Mark Barnes challenges us to re-think the notion of assigning traditional grades. Full of helpful examples and tips for success,* Assessment 3.0 *offers a feedback model that is differentiated, student-focused, and results-oriented.*"

—William Sterrett, Educational Leadership Faculty Member and Program Coordinator, Author of *Insights into Action.*

Mark Barnes is a thoughtful, reflective, practicing educator and a prolific writer. In this book he is able to make a solid case for doing away with grades as we have come to understand them over the centuries. Many educators struggle with grades and their effect on true learning, and Mark underscores the many reasons for this. He puts in place a plan to eliminate grades and empower learning as a result. His 21st century approach to meaningful assessment is a breath of fresh air to educators who are tired of hearing from anyone but educators as to what assessment should be. In this book Mark explains the history of assessment, describes why it is not working, and provides a strategy to change from what we are doing with assessment to what we as educators should be doing in regard to meaningful assessment. This may be the jumpstart needed to get a meaningful and long overdue dialogue started.

—Tom Whitby, co-author of *The Relevant Educator*

Assessment 3.0

*Throw Out Your Grade Book
and Inspire Learning*

Mark Barnes

CORWIN
A SAGE Company

FOR INFORMATION:

Corwin

A SAGE Company

2455 Teller Road

Thousand Oaks, California 91320

(800) 233-9936

www.corwin.com

SAGE Publications Ltd.

1 Oliver's Yard

55 City Road

London EC1Y 1SP

United Kingdom

SAGE Publications India Pvt. Ltd.

B 1/I 1 Mohan Cooperative Industrial Area

Mathura Road, New Delhi 110 044

India

SAGE Publications Asia-Pacific Pte. Ltd.

3 Church Street

#10-04 Samsung Hub

Singapore 049483

Printed in the United States of America.

A catalog record of this book is available from the Library of Congress.

ISBN: 9781483373881

This book is printed on acid-free paper.

Acquisitions Editor: Arnis Burvikovs

Associate Editor: Desirée A. Bartlett

Editorial Assistant: Andrew Olson

Copy Editor: Diane DiMura

Typesetter: C&M Digitals (P) Ltd.

Proofreader: Rae-Ann Goodwin

Indexer: Judy Hunt

Cover Designer: Karine Hovsepian

Marketing Manager: Lisa Lysne

SFI® Certified Sourcing
www.sfiprogram.org
SFI-00453

15 16 17 18 19 10 9 8 7 6 5 4 3 2 1

Contents

Acknowledgments   ix

About the Author   xiii

Introduction   1

Chapter 1. The Trouble With Assessment 2.0   7
    The I'm-a-Failure Mentality   9
    Grades Are Carrots and Sticks   10
    It's Impossible to Distinguish an A From a C   12
    The Math Does Not Compute   14
    The GPA Is a Tail Wagging the Dog   15
    The Community College Effect   17
    The Undeniable Truth   18

Chapter 2. When 2 + 2 Doesn't Equal 4   21
    The 100-Point Conundrum   22
    The Prezi Project   24
    Tests and Numbers   28

Chapter 3. SE2R—A Formula for Change   31
    Rebuilding Assessment   32
    SE2R: An Overview   34
    Class Assignment   34
    Summarize   35
    Explain   36
    Redirect and Resubmit   37
    SE2R in High School   40

Chapter 4. Coppell Middle School East   45
    The Pilot Team   46
    A Difficult Transition   46

Christina   47
Assessment Without Comparison   48
Tori   49
Improving Feedback, Increasing Achievement   52
The Numbers That Matter   55

Chapter 5. Involving Students   **59**
The Danger of Too Much Written Feedback   61
SE2R Shorthand   62
Yes, You Have Time for Feedback   64
The SE2R Portfolio   67
Talking About Feedback   70
Report Card Time: Now What?   72
Performance Review   75

Chapter 6. Feedback in a Digital World   **81**
Giving Students What They Want   83
Feedback Tools That Engage Learners   84
    The Blog   85
    Social Networks   87
    Mobile Devices and Applications   89
Content Curation and Feedback   90

Chapter 7. Tips for Success   **95**
A Proactive Approach   96
Explain How It Works to Students   97
Talk to Administrators   97
A Letter to Parents   99
Continue the Conversation   100
Celebrate Independent Learning   103
Evaluate Your Approach   104

Conclusion   **107**

Appendices
Appendix A: Feedback From the Field   111
Appendix B: SE2R Feedback Quick-Reference Guide   117
Appendix C: SE2R Feedback You Can Use Today   121

References   **125**

Index   **129**

Acknowledgments

U nlike many authors I don't have a list of teachers who influenced me to become an educator. It wasn't until I tried various jobs that I realized I wanted to be a teacher, and many years passed before I understood what effective teaching and learning was. I'll acknowledge some of the professionals who influenced my teaching philosophy throughout this book. There are a few individuals, though, who merit mentioning here.

In other books I've written, I've acknowledged my wife, Mollie, at the end in sort of a last-but-not-least statement of honor. For this book, it's important to acknowledge Mollie first. Because she is the most influential person in my life, I'm not sure I would have ever transformed my classroom and my teaching methods as I did if she hadn't endorsed the move. When I explained to her one summer how I wanted to discard every traditional technique I'd ever used in favor of a unique combination of progressive teaching methods I'd studied for months, she smiled and said, "I think it's amazing and courageous that you're willing to change everything so you can help kids. You should do it." Without Mollie this book would not exist. She is so much more than my wife and mother to my children. She is my best friend and my most cherished confidant.

My son Ethan and my daughter Lauren watch me spend countless hours sitting at the computer when they prefer that I spend time with them. They compensate by asking me about my work. "Which book are you working on, daddy? How many words is it? Where is that picture going?" I appreciate their patience and the precious time we steal together, even when I'm racing toward deadlines. They are the primary reason I want to change education.

While it sounds cliché, there are not enough ways to say thank you to the remarkable educators at Coppell East Middle School. The courage and care they exhibit daily is unparalleled in the profession. A special thanks to Kat, Laura, and Megan. They know why. I appreciate the mighty efforts of Gerald Aungst, Dr. Charlie Gleek, John Romanoff, Mike Fisher, Dr. Stacy Reeves, Joy Kirr, Michelle Baldwin, Garnett Hillman, Shelly Terrell, Hadley Ferguson, Laura Springer, and the many students and parents who have shared their insights.

I owe so much to the patient, professional people at Corwin Press, especially Ariel Price and Arnis Burvikovs. They showed unwavering faith in this project, and Ariel helped me find my voice, which sometimes gets lost in a maelstrom of ideas. Thank you, Diane DiMura, for your acute attention to detail.

I appreciate all of the dedicated members of the Teachers Throwing Out Grades Facebook group, and the Assessment 3.0 Facebook page. When I needed help with research, they were my first, and most reliable, source. And when it comes to legitimate education reform, they are the most dedicated educators I know.

Publisher's Acknowledgments

Corwin gratefully acknowledges the contributions of the following reviewers:

D. Allan Bruner, National Board Certified Teacher
Chemistry Teacher and Science Chair
Colton High School
Colton, OR

Diane Callahan
Retired 7th/8th Grade Science Teacher
Fairfield Middle School
Fairfield, OH

Tamara Daugherty
3rd Grade Teacher
Lakeville Elementary
Apopka, FL

Shelly Miedona
District Title I Resource Teacher
Indian River Schools
Vero Beach, FL

About the Author

 **Mark Barnes** is a veteran classroom teacher, education consultant, and author of the critically acclaimed *Role Reversal: Achieving Uncommonly Excellent Results in the Student-Centered Classroom* (2013), *The 5-Minute Teacher* (2013), *Teaching the iStudent* (2014), and *5 Skills for the Global Learner* (2015). A longtime adjunct professor at two Ohio colleges, Mark has created five online courses on web-based instruction, mobile learning, and using Twitter in the classroom and as a professional development tool. A leading expert on student-centered learning, Mark has helped thousands of educators build digitally enhanced, project-based, no-grades classrooms. Mark is the creator of the internationally recognized how-to video site for educators Learn It in 5 and publisher of the popular education blog *Brilliant or Insane: Education on the Edge* (*B or I*). Named a Top 10 education technology blog by *EdTech Magazine* in 2014, *B or I* inspires hundreds of thousands of loyal readers. Mark's Facebook group, Teachers Throwing Out Grades, is a growing collection of educators dedicated to changing the way learning is assessed, and this group helped launch the often-trending #TTOG Twitter chat. Mark can be found sharing information and articles about best practices in education daily on Twitter at @markbarnes19.

In memory of the suffragettes. They taught us that even when something has lasted for centuries, if it's wrong it must be vanquished.

Introduction

Life is a series of natural and spontaneous changes.
Don't resist them—that only creates sorrow. Let reality
be reality. Let things flow naturally forward in whatever
way they like.

—Lao Tzu, Chinese philosopher

I f teachers were surveyed about who has had the biggest
impact on education, it's unlikely that James Pillans would
land near the top of the list. He might not make it at all.
Despite Pillans' relative anonymity, he dramatically changed
teaching and learning. In 1801, Pillans invented the blackboard and colored chalk, education tools that have endured
for more than 200 years. Sure, many teachers have gravitated
away from chalk and slate to Interactive whiteboards and tablet computers, but Pillans' centuries-old invention remains a
staple in classrooms worldwide. What made Pillans' idea so
revolutionary is that it provided a simple solution to an
imposing problem. "Teachers had no way to present a lesson
or a problem to the class as a whole; instead they had to go to
each individual student and write a problem or assignment on
each one's slate" (Concordia Online Education, 2012). Enter
Pillans, who taught geography at the Old High School in
Edinburgh, and his blackboard, which gave students a new
visual world of learning.

Pillans' blackboard revolutionized instruction.

If James Pillans could impact education for hundreds of years with a blackboard and chalk, isn't it possible that another absurdly simple idea can revolutionize education for the next two hundred years? Modern education needs a modest solution to an even more grievous problem—measuring learning with numbers, percentages, and letters. Like those 200-year-old slates, traditional grades have been the norm for so long that they aren't often questioned, yet they continue to leave cavernous potholes on the road to achievement and independent learning. Ask students what they've learned or tell them to assess themselves and most respond with blank stares. When students can't assess their own learning and understanding of what they have or have not mastered, this is a titanic problem that must be fixed. The good news is this important issue can be rectified with James-Pillans-type simplicity. Assessment 3.0 is today's blackboard, and it can modernize teaching and learning without inventions or manufacturing costs.

I know this because I've experienced this revolution in my own classroom, and I've witnessed many teachers across America and in other countries make the transition away from grades. It took years for me to comprehend the deleterious effects of grades. When I began my career as a classroom teacher more than 20 years ago, I was convinced that teaching was about lecture, worksheets, homework, tests, and grades. Evaluation was reduced to simple math. Students scored points on various activities; I added the numbers, calculated a percentage, and placed a letter grade on a report card. These were my methods for a very long time, and a host of students struggled to excel because of them.

Reflecting on this horrible injustice, it struck me that I was not alone. In fact, most teachers back then and, unfortunately, many today continue to teach in this old-fashioned way. Even renowned education researcher and author Carol Ann Tomlinson needed time to recognize her own faulty approach. "My metamorphosis in coming to understand what effective use of assessment looked like and ultimately appreciating its great potential to enhance teaching and learning was glacially slow" (Tomlinson & Moon, 2013, p. x). After more than a decade of inundating students with homework and worksheets and returning their work with only numbers and letters scrawled at the top, I converted my classroom into what I call a Results Only Learning Environment—a vibrant, joyous, somewhat chaotic place, filled with enthusiastic learners. The tantalizing part of this exciting classroom is the complete elimination of any kind of measurement of learning. Numbers, percentages, and letters disappeared from students' activities, projects, and even tests. The results-only classroom contains lively conversations about learning and descriptive narrative feedback, and students are given the chance to revisit prior learning and make changes to their work in order to demonstrate mastery. Some people believe a classroom without grades to be impossible, but the research and my experience prove otherwise.

THE ARGUMENT

The primary purpose of this book is to convince educators and parents around the world that eliminating traditional grades is not only possible but is, in fact, necessary if we are to evolve beyond the archaic measurements that stifle learning. Throughout the book, I will argue for not just more formative assessment but for assessment that is based on a routine formula that both teacher and student use daily to critique learning. This formula is called SE2R. The abbreviation stands for Summarize, Explain, Redirect, Resubmit. Although it may look like something intended for a math or science class, SE2R is designed to appraise learning in any subject and at any grade level. The influence of SE2R is remarkable, considering its simplicity. This formula is the foundation of Assessment 3.0, a system that may seem improbable but contains a truth that teachers, administrators, and parents can no longer ignore: Measuring learning is education's principal problem—one that stunts the growth of our students even more than a lack of technology, oversized classrooms, and standardized testing. SE2R generates an ongoing conversation about learning, leading to mastery of concepts and skills in a way that traditional grades cannot.

The transition to teaching without grades is no small task, as it requires rejecting an established model that has dominated education virtually since its inception. To support this appeal for major education reform, I will argue throughout this book that number and letter grades are not only wholly subjective, they are immaterial when it comes to understanding what students have and have not accomplished in an academic setting. The goal is to convince you that attempting to measure achievement is a fruitless endeavor that reveals nothing about learning and, far more disconcerting, disdains the opinion of the student. In order to ascertain any substantive understanding of what students accomplish in an academic setting, a two-way dialogue is necessary; you will see what this dialogue looks like and how it impacts learning and motivation in various places throughout the book.

Along the way, I'll share my history with both traditional and progressive education, but more important, I will share the astonishing stories of teachers, principals, parents, and students who have experienced a no-grades classroom and SE2R feedback and are unwilling to return to an environment where learning is built on the blind subjectivity of grades. The results they have realized demonstrate that education without grades is not only necessary but also realistic. What about admission to college, you may wonder. How can students be evaluated without a GPA? College deans and professors will share alternative ways for evaluating students for admission, and I'll explain the *community college effect,* a theory, built on some interesting research and a hypothesis, suggesting that the achievements of junior college students offer strong support for eliminating traditional grades. This book isn't only about research and anecdotes. There are strategies for providing meaningful narrative feedback, for using technology for assessment, for creating significant conversations about achievement and, perhaps most important, for teaching students to be self-evaluative, independent learners.

BREAKING BARRIERS

Assessment 3.0 has its barriers, four of which will be addressed throughout this book. First, administrators are bound by policy and aren't comfortable with sweeping change. Therefore, understanding how to integrate a feedback model, while appeasing school leaders, who likely will not embrace radical reform, is critical. Second, until traditional report cards are abolished (I believe that one day they will be), final grades should be a conversation between teacher and student. If a mark is required for a report card, let's ask our students what they believe that grade should be, based on a detailed assessment by both student and teacher of all that was or was not accomplished during a grading period. Third, parents are accustomed to grades. Some of education's most important stakeholders, parents can push back pretty hard when they don't see numbers or letters on their children's work. Because parents only understand grades, moving away from what I call assessment 2.0 can be a bigger mountain to climb for parents than it is for teachers. Fourth, and most daunting, is the barrier of time and tradition. Resistance to major reform is easy, when people rely on the "that's-the-way-we've-always-done-it" refrain.

WHAT ABOUT ACCOUNTABILITY?

We live in an era of standardization, accountability, and high stakes testing. I've encountered teachers in the field who read my first education book, *Role Reversal* (Barnes, 2013), which introduces SE2R and the elimination of grades. Many of them love the philosophy behind narrative feedback but suggest that it's impossible to fully implement, due to the accountability measures and standardized testing that dominate today's schools. "Even if I believe that grades are punitive, how do I get around them?" is a typical question. The short answer is not always well received because it offers no plan. "You just do it because our greatest responsibility is to kids," I've often said. "Measuring learning with numbers and letters is inherently wrong, and it has to stop." I've realized over the past few years that a different, more profound, response to this concern is necessary. The deeper dive and, hopefully, silver bullet answer to embracing Assessment 3.0 is contained in this book.

Many teachers have already thrown out their grade books. They are using SE2R, which is discussed in full detail in Chapter 3. Others have nudged grades closer to the wastebasket, choosing strategies like standards-based grading that mimic SE2R in one way or another. Assessment 3.0 is, I believe, the boldest example of education reform that we've ever seen, and the one that will forever change teaching and learning. So, before dismissing the idea as outlandish or as something an administrator won't allow, consider the case studies, models, strategies, and tips in this book. In the end, you may completely alter how you assess learning, or you might simply fine-tune what you currently do. Either way, you will be part of a transformation that will impact students now and forever.

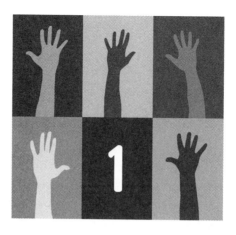

The Trouble With Assessment 2.0

Because measuring the results of rote learning is easy, rote prevails. What kids know is just not important in comparison with whether they can think.

> —Sugata Mitra, education professor, known for the "Hole in the Wall" experiment

For more than a decade as a classroom teacher, I placed number and letter grades on my students' papers and projects. Activities were assigned values, as randomly and thoughtlessly as one might select a flavor of ice cream for a Sunday afternoon dessert. Why did I treat my students' hard work with such disregard? The answer is simple, if sad. I didn't know any better; that's the way I'd always done it, and I wasn't aware of another way. Students had to be graded, and this occurred with points, percentages, and letters.

> The GPA is quite possibly the most dangerous tool in education.

As a preservice teacher in the early 1990s, I learned to evaluate learning, using assessment 2.0. The 90s and early 2000s were rife with many things 2.0, which in general terms meant an upgrade or the next iteration of something. First, we had the World Wide Web; then we had Web 2.0, which included online collaboration and social media. Web 3.0 involves content curation and cloud computing. Keep this vocabulary in mind throughout this chapter, aimed at combatting common arguments in favor of assessment 2.0, which is all about measuring learning. "By the 1930s, the ABC approach had been adopted by a wide group of schools and universities around the country and, not coincidentally, would be reabsorbed by a number of industrial interests, including dairy, beef, poultry, and plywood" (Thomsen, 2013). In the ABC approach, which thrives in classrooms around the world today, everything students do is given a point value, which translates to a percentage and ultimately to a letter grade. Each letter grade has an attached numeric value, and at the end of a marking period, all of the grades a student receives and their respective numeric values are calculated into a grade point average (GPA). The GPA is quite possibly the most dangerous tool in education. It places a subjective label on students that says very little about academic achievement.

I was taught assessment 2.0 during my time as a student teacher and employed it routinely in my classroom. That's the way it had been done for as long as the 30-year veterans in my school had taught and, likely, for 30 years prior to their arrival. Why does this ancient strategy continue, without much consideration? Kentucky professor Thomas Guskey (2011) says this of grades: "They've been a part of our education experiences for so long that they usually go unquestioned, despite the fact that they are ineffective and potentially harmful to students." Melissa Harris-Perry, a professor of political science at Tulane, began considering a different assessment model years ago, suggesting that grades distract students from exploring what is valuable. Instead, she suggests that students concern themselves more with the opinions of a single person or a small group: "What would happen if students were free to experience classes, retain information and build connections without fear that their futures hung in the balance of a single imperfect product?" (Harris-Perry, 2012).

It took one particularly disturbing school year, when half of my 120 students failed language arts, for me to begin posing the kinds of questions that Harris-Perry asked. After a summer of research and reflection, I rebuilt myself as a teacher. The most amazing change was the complete elimination of number and letter grades from all activities and projects, with the support of the school administration. We'll discuss grading reforms and acceptance from educators at many levels later. This was a bold undertaking, based on some key research by several luminaries in education, psychology, and other fields and the realization that the way we assess learning doesn't work. One of education's most successful and prolific authors, Alfie Kohn, says grades tend to reduce students' interest in learning and their desire to take on challenging tasks. Kohn (1999) rejects grades because they detract from the quality of students' thinking, all while being invalid and unreliable as a means for evaluating achievement. Daniel Pink studied motivation for years prior to writing *Drive: The Surprising Truth About What Motivates Us*. Pink (2009) likens grades to extrinsic motivators, which deprive children of the autonomy and sense of purpose that all human beings covet. "Good grades are a reward for compliance but don't have much to do with learning. Meanwhile, students whose grades don't measure up often see themselves as failures and give up trying to learn" (p. 176).

THE I'M-A-FAILURE MENTALITY

Pink's argument that grades make students feel that they don't measure up resonated with me. Many of my students gave up on learning after a steady stream of zeroes and failing grades devastated their confidence. Some even stopped working entirely. "Why should I do it?" a reluctant learner asked one day. "I'll fail anyway." Upon hearing this declaration, I turned to a counselor for advice, only to learn that the student had a history of report cards littered with F's. "He's used to failing, so he doesn't try anymore," was a refrain that became too familiar. Prior to that discussion with the guidance counselor, it was incomprehensible that a student would not even attempt an activity or project. What I would have, in the past, perceived to be laziness or poor parenting turned out to be fear of continuing failure. This epiphany coupled with the research I did during the subsequent summer helped me realize that the profession I loved was deeply troubled. Many people say there's no magic wand in education. I always believed this to be true, until I stopped grading and saw even the most reluctant learners take on all activities.

GRADES ARE CARROTS AND STICKS

The devil's advocate who might agree that grades fail reluctant learners will argue that grades motivate high achievers. While the student who eyes admission to an Ivy League school appears to work for good grades, it is more accurate to say that she is driven by fear of the low grade, which lessens the desire to learn for the sake of learning. "Conventional wisdom tells us we grade students to artificially induce their intrinsic motivation to strive for the reward of a high grade or to avoid the punishment of a low grade" (Bower, 2013, p. 157). Dozens of past students, many of whom I caught cheating, claimed they'd be met with ghastly punishment at home if they made low grades. In effect, grades become a weapon, not much different from the threat of a spanking that a child might experience if he doesn't stop harassing his sister. Once threatened with bodily harm, he may refrain from pulling her hair but, in most cases, the boy's change in behavior is more out of fear of physical pain than it is because he knows that pulling his sister's hair is wrong. This same carrot-and-stick approach to education encourages bad study habits as well as cheating.

Unfortunately, many modern educators still use grades like the paddles that teachers wielded back in the day of corporal punishment. The threat of a bad grade may not make a student cringe in fear of a stinging backside, but the long-term effect of using grades as manipulators is much worse. When students complete worksheets and work book activities that they do not value or, worse, copy from their friends just to acquire a so-called good grade, they fail to experience what is truly important in education—a love of learning. When high achievers don't love learning, they may never reach their true potential and, in many cases, may take short cuts in an effort to meet academic goals. Their counterparts, reluctant learners, who are punished by grades, not only don't love learning, they grow to despise it. This hatred of learning has far-reaching ramifications. "Since it's overwhelmingly poor students who

Photo by Cheryl Casey, thinkstockphotos.com.

Traditional grades frustrate students.

are prone to bad grades, a self-reinforcing loop is created. Poverty leads to bad grades and low self-esteem, which leads to more poverty and social dysfunction" (Thomsen, 2013, p. 1). Amplifying this point, author and education consultant Mike Fisher (2014) equates grades to walls that block the road to learning. "That wall is easily built but nearly impossible to tear down. Kids that experience negative and punitive grading situations in lower grade levels begin to believe that this is their worth and do not aspire to do better because they see no light at the end of the tunnel that was dug for them but that they cannot escape." Future chapters illustrate how meaningful narrative feedback helps reluctant learners tear down the wall that Fisher speaks of and inspires high achievers, taking short cuts to "good" grades to realize their full potential.

It's Impossible to Distinguish an A From a C

Another problem with assessment 2.0 is labeling a child as an *A student*, a *C student*, a *D student*, and so on. Teachers who judge students based on an amalgam of work that has consistently received a similar grade are prone to this kind of labeling. There are many problems with labeling, chief among them failing to properly assess learning, due to the misconception that a student will ultimately reach the same outcome, regardless of the quality of the work the student submits. For example, most people would say there is a significant difference between an A student and a C student. While these marks may suggest that students are excellent and average, respectively, it is conceivable that, in terms of achievement, they are similar, even identical. Conversely, they might be reversed in their abilities—the C student being excellent and the A student being average. It's difficult to tell, using A and C labels because, in reality, both measures are entirely subjective. If education policymakers considered this statement to be true, even for a second, we might see the kind of far-reaching change that I'm suggesting in this book.

How is it possible, you may wonder, for grades to be subjective if they are based on an accumulation of points and percentages? Consider the following scenario, based on this grading approach:

1. The teacher creates an activity.

2. The teacher assigns an arbitrary point value to the activity (10, 20, 100, or even 1,000); these values are typically a derivative of the overall points a student can amass in a grading period, also prescribed by the teacher.

3. The teacher decides how points are acquired on particular tasks using a rubric, points per item within the activity, or gut feeling.

4. Based on one of the evaluation methods in step 3, the activity receives a final score.

5. The final score is translated to a percentage and a corresponding letter grade.

A math teacher assigns a test containing 30 problems. One student thrives in these situations, while an equally proficient mathematician has test anxiety and prefers problems that require real-world application. (Remember what Daniel Pink says about autonomy and motivation; people want to do things when they're given choices.) The student who enjoys tests answers 27 of the 30 problems correctly—good for 90% and a grade of A. Her classmate completes 23 problems correctly and scores 77% for a grade of C. Four problems separate two students who otherwise exhibit relatively identical aptitudes for math. This becomes a pattern throughout the school year, and one becomes an A student and the other a C student.

Oftentimes, in cases like these, the A student is elevated to an advanced class the following year, while the C student is relegated to a "regular" class. Tracking is a by-product of traditional grading and a system that falsely labels students.

Assume, though, that the two students in this scenario are placed in the same math class the following year. Instead of assessment centered on tests, students apply what they know to projects that mimic the kind of math an engineer or architect uses. The C student is overjoyed, as this is her strength. The A student scuffles, because she is not good at abstract thinking. At the end of the year, their grades are reversed. Who, in reality, is excellent, and who is average? In the grade world, this is one problem that can't be solved.

THE MATH DOES NOT COMPUTE

The arbitrariness of the points and percentages that teachers attach to class work has perplexed me for years. It never did in the past because I didn't give it much thought. As most of my colleagues did, I simply decided how many points there would be in a grading period. Then, I separated this unsavory points pie into categories, such as tests, quizzes, homework, bell work, assignments, and projects. These categories were weighted. For example, if I decided there were 1,000 points in a marking period, tests might be 400 of those points. Our one project would eat up 200 more, and the remaining, purportedly less valuable, activities would account for the other 400 points. Keep in mind that when I converted my class into what I call a Results Only Learning Environment, I threw out most of these activities because they had little, if any, connection to learning; most were assigned only as a means for depositing points into our grade book. When teachers decide that a marking period consists of 1,000 points, they must assign activities so students can amass those points. This was quite logical to me for many years.

When grades became obsolete in my class, it occurred to me that there was, indeed, never any logic to the numbers and weights. Why have 1,000 points in a quarter? Why not 500 or 10,000? Should a five-minute bell work activity be valued the same as a homework assignment because both required the same amount of effort? Or was the homework more valuable because it had to be done outside of school? What if some students spent 20 minutes on homework? They would receive the same 10 points as students who completed the activity in five minutes. If my 200-point project has seven parts, how much is each one worth? Do some have more value than others? There is no reasonable answer to these questions, but this issue of weighting will be examined further in Chapter 2.

The GPA Is a Tail Wagging the Dog

Many educators are willing to eliminate measuring students with numbers and letters, once they learn how easily it can be done. Still, other barriers obstruct the path leading away from grades and to an assessment system centered on conversation and narrative feedback. In most cases, any trepidation about abolishing grades directly correlates to worry over how students will be admitted to college if they don't have a grade point average and a high school class rank. This is a reasonable fear and a setback that must be overcome with a grassroots effort (more on this later). The K–12 education world can no longer allow colleges and universities to dictate policy. This is tantamount to the tail wagging the dog, and it has to stop.

> Perhaps the day has come for all universities to wave the entrance requirement of minimum GPA and allow students to work hard for success.
>
> —Dr. Stacy Reeves, University of Southern Mississippi

Turning things around will be easy when college admission deans realize that high school educators are unwilling to send students off to the postsecondary world, equipped with only GPAs and SAT scores. Many college administrators have already figured out that GPAs have very little meaning in terms of the value a student brings to their school. According to Mary Beth Marklein's (2013) *USA Today* article, some

American colleges "barely look at an applicant's GPA. 'It's meaningless,' says Greg Roberts, admissions dean at the University of Virginia." While noteworthy that a highly ranked state school like Virginia would disdain the GPA when admitting new students, even more impressive is the philosophy of a college like Swarthmore, ranked at the top of *Princeton Review's* best-value private colleges list in 2013. Swarthmore admissions dean, Jim Brock, declares grade point average, "useless," as a means of evaluating candidates for admission. In fact, Swarthmore doesn't even offer GPA calculations for guidebook publishers (Marklein, 2013). Another well-known private college, Wellesley, recently began what they term *shadow grading*, which means that freshmen in their first semester earn pass or fail marks. This change in grading practices came after faculty member Lee Cuba studied the impact of grades on learning and concluded that "academic achievement and engagement are negatively correlated—in other words, the more time students spend thinking about getting an A, the less time they're thinking about what it is they should be learning" (Johnson, 2014). University of Southern Mississippi education professor Dr. Stacy Reeves (2014), who has taught in both K–12 and college classrooms for more than 25 years, puts an even finer point on why it's time for colleges to reconsider GPAs and class rank as factors for college admission:

> Even the most ethical, fair and honest teacher will make the once-a-year mistake which could be reflected in a grade, and if not caught, shows up on the student's GPA. Perhaps that was the difference between a $10,000 and $20,000 scholarship—just one small mistake on one small day. Perhaps the day has come for all universities to wave the entrance requirement of minimum GPA and allow students to work hard for success. The GPA rankings formerly used can be done away with and high school students may be much better measured through current success in their coursework.

THE COMMUNITY COLLEGE EFFECT

Many community colleges have an open admission policy; that is, they accept students with low grades or, in many cases, no grades. Some accept students who do not have a high school diploma. How does this support an argument for eliminating grades? The answer lies in what I call the *community college effect*. In a report on community colleges on their 100th birthday, Richard Coley of the Educational Testing Service provides some telling data about students attending two-year schools.

A large portion of the research might lead one to conclude that community colleges are nothing more than a refuge for poor students, both academically and socioeconomically. Grades are meaningless to these students, one could argue. Most have

> It is fair to conclude that the journey from the K–12 world to adulthood and to the job market involves far more than grades.

made low grades throughout their K–12 lives and few move on to four-year colleges, so they didn't need high GPAs in the first place. Alternatively, consider this supposition: If grades and GPAs are about ranking, and if ranking is designed to help students get into the best colleges, then students with high GPAs who land at the top of their classes, presumably, will attend top-ranked colleges and ultimately attain the best jobs. If the supposition were false, why would students strive for high marks and work so hard to be valedictorian?

Enter the community college effect. As Coley's research indicates, the majority of students in community college enter with very low GPAs, or none at all. While only about one-fourth transfer to four-year colleges, those who do matriculate perform surprisingly well in the professional world. "Evidence suggests that when community college students transfer to four-year colleges and complete their bachelor's degrees, they are about as competitive in the labor market as similar students who start at four-year colleges" (Coley, 2000). Laurence Emmanuelle Hadjas is a perfect example of Coley's research and the community college effect. Hadjas, originally from Algeria, dropped out of high school, before moving to the United States, where she acquired her GED. She then attended a community college in Philadelphia, where she flourished. Hadjas became a mother, which she says contributed to her maturation and a new appreciation for learning. "What made me successful, I would say, is a combination of teachers and personal attitude and being a mother of a child with a disability" (Hadjas, 2014). Based on this evidence, it is fair to conclude that the journey from the K–12 world to adulthood and to the job market involves far more than grades. If students like Hadjas can struggle academically in high school, then attend a junior college, and then transfer to a four-year school and perform as well as their peers who began at high-quality four-year institutions, it stands to reason that both the community college student and the high school valedictorian can complete their paths to the workplace without the intrusion of traditional grades. This is the community college effect, which basically hypothesizes that traditional grades are meaningless when it comes to success in life. A variety of factors, including maturation, teaching styles, parenthood, and environment, contribute to the overall growth of a student. And while some students struggle in high school, they may, in fact, perform very well later in life—as well as high school valedictorians. Furthermore, if there's any validity to the community college effect, grades, GPAs, and class rank are completely irrelevant factors when evaluating students for admission to college. Thus, they are also irrelevant factors for assessing learning in the K–12 world.

THE UNDENIABLE TRUTH

The grades or no grades debate is intriguing. For evidence of this, look at the TED conversation I started in 2011 on the subject, which inspired hundreds of comments from people all around the world (Barnes, 2011). Many said they love the idea of schools without grades, while others remained skeptical.

Exhilarating as it was, the TED conversation is admittedly tall on opinion and short on research. This admission notwithstanding, the evidence against traditional grades and in favor of feedback does exist and is quite overwhelming. "Research experiments have established that, while student learning can be advanced by feedback through comments, the giving of numerical scores or grades has a negative effect, in that students ignore comments when marks are also given. These results often surprise teachers, but those who have abandoned the giving of marks discover that their experience confirms the findings: students do engage more productively in improving their work" (Black, Harrison, Lee, Marshall, & Wiliam, 2004, p. 13). It has also been reported that grades depress creativity, instill a fear of failure and, even worse, decrease students' interest in learning (Butler & Nisan, 1986).

In their research of assessment, former Virginia teacher of the year Carol Ann Tomlinson and international consultant and researcher Tonya Moon (2013) identify three ways that grading impedes learning:

> First, it misrepresents the learning process to students, leading them to conclude that making errors is cause for punishment rather than an opportunity to improve. Second, it focuses students more on getting good grades than on learning. Third, it makes the classroom environment seem unsafe for many students—and would make it seem unsafe to more students if classwork were appropriately challenging for the full range of learners. (p. 62)

Grades also encourage competition among students, deemphasizing learning. "Students given feedback as marks are likely to see it as a way to compare themselves with others (ego involvement); those given only comments see it as helping them to improve (task involvement). The latter group outperforms the former" (Black et al., 2004, p. 18). Most telling is the work of John Hattie and Helen Timperly, university professors and researchers specializing in assessment strategies and best practices in the classroom. In *The Power of Feedback* (2007), Hattie and

Timperly summarize exhaustive research, including Hattie's review of 500 meta-analyses, comprising 180,000 studies of nearly 40 million students on more than 100 areas that impact achievement. Not only does the research put feedback near the top of the list of items that positively influence achievement, student self-grading, discussed in various places throughout this book, is Number 1 on Hattie's list.

Despite the continuing use of traditional number and letter grades, the arguments against assessment 2.0 prove that it's time for a dramatic change in how we assess learning. Colleges are already admitting students without grades, and the community college effect demonstrates that students with either no grades or poor grades, who pursue education beyond their first two years, eventually perform as well as their four-year college peers. Finally, the research indicating that traditional grades negatively impact performance for all learners is ubiquitous and valid. These and other factors mentioned in this chapter confirm that number and letter grades impede learning. At the very least, this evidence should raise enough doubt in all educators to consider an alternative to traditional grading. That method is Assessment 3.0.

REFLECTION

- What do you think are the biggest barriers to eliminating traditional grades?
- Describe students you consider to be A students. What motivates them?
- Now, describe students you'd call D students. What do you believe motivates them?
- Draw a middle line on a paper and list a typical A student on one side and D student on the other. Can you list their characteristics? How are they different and how are they similar?

It may be helpful to discuss this with colleagues. If you are an administrator, consider this topic as part of a faculty or department meeting. This collaboration builds a grassroots movement away from traditional assessment. I'll discuss the power of the grassroots movement later.

When 2 + 2 Doesn't Equal 4

You know, I'm fairly intelligent, but I don't think my grades reflected that.

—Barry Sanders, former professional football player

G rades lie. I believe this statement to be indisputable. In an attempt to convince all educators, parents, and policymakers, even those who remain steadfast in the belief that schools cannot exist without some kind of measurements, I shared research and practical experience in Chapter 1 that emphasizes the value of feedback over grades. The teachers at Coppell Middle School East (Chapter 4) supply evidence of more than 300 students who have adapted easily to a no-grades system and have flourished. There is support indicating that students in an environment built on feedback, conversation, and self-evaluation outperform their peers in traditional classrooms on standardized tests. While it can be argued that the community college effect is hypothetical, it certainly fosters enough doubt in grades to give college admissions deans plenty of reason to change their evaluation policies. For the naysayers who continue to question the validity of no-grades assessment, this chapter examines classroom scenarios that demonstrate how the numbers don't add up.

THE 100 POINT CONUNDRUM

On an unseasonably warm winter morning in Boston, 50 teachers, principals, and administrators, representing more than 10 states and countries, huddled in small groups in a hotel conference room. They were engaged in a heated debate about grades. As the workshop leader, I presented them with an example of a class assignment with a point value of 100. The students, the audience was informed, had completed a review of conflict in fiction, which included "person vs. person, vs. self, and vs. society." In the brief lesson, students reviewed excerpts from different novels and analyzed each conflict and how it might impact decisions the main character made. Then students were asked to complete both parts of this assignment:

1. Identify parts of the story that contain each of the conflicts we've studied. For example, write, "In Chapter 2, page 14, a person vs. X conflict occurs when . . . "

2. Explain how the main character reacts to or resolves each conflict, using evidence from the story.

In the interest of time, I gave an example of feedback a teacher could deliver based on how one student handled the assignment.

"Robert, you have clearly identified two of the three conflicts we studied and summarized how they appear in the novel. However, you gave no explanation of how the main character reacts to the conflicts."

I set a timer to five minutes and instructed the audience to discuss the activity and how it was handled and to determine a score for Robert. As the clock ticked, the volume of the conversation rose. Groups of five or six struggled to agree on a grade. The teachers defended their opinions vehemently. "He did half the assignment, so it has to be 50/100," one said. "He didn't even complete half," someone chimed in from a nearby table, as the discussion spilled from one group to the next. One attendee suggested that the second part of the activity should be worth more points than the first, because there is higher level thinking involved with explaining a character's conflict resolution, whereas simply identifying the conflict is at the bottom of Bloom's Taxonomy. So, she argued, since Robert left that portion out completely, he should receive no higher than 30 or 35 points. Not surprisingly, others argued that the first instruction was worth more, for numerous reasons, so Robert should receive 60 or 65 points of the possible 100.

A song rang out from the computer, indicating that the timer had reached zero. Thirty more seconds passed, before silence settled on the room. Only three of the nine groups agreed on a score for Robert. Two believed he should receive a final mark of 40/100, arguing that he did less than half of the activity. Six educators at another table scored the work at 55/100. They reasoned that part one should be valued higher, because it contained less opinion than part two. Since Robert omitted one of the three conflicts, he would be penalized five points. This decision received pushback from several individuals around the room, who concluded that if part one was worth 60 of the points, and there are three conflicts, it stands to reason that each conflict would be worth 20 points. If Robert identified only two, he should score 40/100. This logic was applauded by some and rejected by others. "Is it possible that Robert understands all three conflicts and could easily respond to the second prompt?" I wondered out loud. Some attendees said, "Of course." Others said "No, or he would have finished the activity." The correct response, I believe, is that Robert is certainly able to complete the entire assignment and demonstrate understanding of conflict in fiction. There may be several legitimate reasons that the activity is incomplete. When Robert is given a grade, which the workshop discussion clearly indicates is subjective and punitive, and no conversation about learning occurs, it is unclear why he didn't complete the work or if he comprehends the learning outcome. Perhaps Robert had an off day. Maybe he was ill or confused and too shy to seek help. He may have been distracted and simply forgot to finish all parts of the assignment. The evidence against this kind of assessment is overwhelming, but this is a language arts assignment, and these can always leave room for subjectivity. Math, though, is something entirely different. The answer is either right or wrong. Or is it?

THE PREZI PROJECT

Some math teachers envision their subject as being all about the numbers. However, like the social sciences, there is a place for conversation about learning in math. Like the writing assignment example in the prior section, the following math example magnifies the subjective nature of grades and the objectivity of feedback, even in a math class.

John Romanoff is a middle school math teacher in a suburb of Cleveland, Ohio. Considered one of his district's technology experts, Romanoff started integrating websites and media into his lessons long before most math teachers ever dreamed of the possibility. A few years ago, Romanoff created a project, in which students would demonstrate learning by building a digital slide show using Prezi, a web-based presentation tool. This is quite a departure from the textbooks and worksheets that continue to dominate today's garden-variety math class. The Prezi project guidelines instruct students to create a presentation that illustrates what they know about simplifying and solving various types of linear equations. A progressive-minded teacher at a traditional school, Romanoff created a rubric, which contains a checklist of project activities and corresponding point values (Figure 2.1). He assigned 35 points to the section on solving

| Figure 2.1 | The Prezi Project |

Your final project for chapter three is a presentation on simplifying and solving various types of linear equations. Below is the rubric for this project. This project is worth 100 points and is graded on grammar, mechanics, accuracy, and visual clarity. Visual clarity means that the slide is not cluttered, and transitions between slides make sense.

PREZI PROJECT RUBRIC

SLIDE	POINTS
Title	
• Name and class period • Project title	**5**
Vocabulary	
Define the following: • inverse operation • reciprocal • like terms • distributive property	**10**
Solving two-step equations	**20**
• Include a worked out example.	✓ 10
• Include a *generic* process that could be followed for any one-or-two-step equation.	✓ 10
Solving multistep equations	**35**
• Include an example of solving an equation in which the distributive property **AND** combining like terms are used **(ONE EQUATION WITH BOTH).**	✓ 15
• Describe the process for applying the distributive property and show an example.	✓ 10
• Describe the process for combining like terms and show an example.	✓ 10
Solving equations with variables on both sides	**30**
• Include an example of solving an equation with variables on both sides of the equal sign.	✓ 15
• Include a *generic* description of how to gather like terms.	✓ 15

Source: Rubric created by John Romanoff.

multistep equations, more than any other part of the project. Solving two-step equations came in third place on the five-part project, at just 20 points.

During a discussion about traditional grading, I told Romanoff about the writing assignment I presented at the workshop in Boston and how attendees were so divided on how it should be scored. Considering their indecisiveness, I wondered if a similar scenario might confound math teachers attempting to grade the same project under slightly altered circumstances. I asked Romanoff to consider two math teachers, in different classes, assigning his Prezi project.

Although the two teachers would assign the project with the same guidelines, what if they were to weight portions of the project differently? There was lengthy contemplation before Romanoff (July 2014) responded.

> I suppose the grade for any part could be adjusted based on how the grader values that part. For me, I appreciate creativity in problem solving, so I place less value on vocabulary. At the same time, I know that a basic understanding of terms is helpful and necessary in math. I also think that the grade could be shifted based on how the grader feels about the student. If the student has made progress and shown growth, I may be inclined to give the student the benefit of the doubt. This is akin to you reading a student's work and "knowing" what she meant with a misplaced apostrophe. What if the writing of that student was well above what she had done all year? The same is true for partial credit in math. If I know a student has worked hard, doesn't he deserve *something?*

Consider the ramifications of math teachers assigning Romanoff's linear equation project but changing the weights of each section, based on their own interpretations. Like

Robert, who received a variety of scores on his conflict activity based on the opinion of teachers who weighted the activity differently, students completing the Prezi project might have similar understanding of linear equations while receiving completely different grades. What if, for example, one teacher weights the vocabulary and two-step equation sections on the rubric (Figure 2.1) at 60 points and applies just 30 total points to multistep equations and equations with variables? This approach leaves 10 points for name and project title. Another teacher designates 30 points for vocabulary and two-step equations, 60 points for the other equation sections and 10 points for name and title.

Here's one potential scenario that highlights this very serious problem. Student A completes the project that emphasizes vocabulary and the two-step equations. Student B completes the project, on which the teacher has assigned higher value to multistep equations and equations with variables. Both students score perfectly on the last two parts of the project. Student A earns just 30 points, while student B earns 60 points. Let's assume both students earn 10 points for name and project title, but they do poorly on vocabulary and two-step equations; in fact, they fail to follow any guidelines on those sections and are given zeroes by their respective teachers. Here are their grades on the Prezi project:

Student A: 40/100, 40%, F

Student B: 70/100, 70%, C

Some might suggest that this example is extreme. Who is to say that the two teachers wouldn't weight the project the same way? This is a fair question but one that amplifies the position that how teachers assess activities and projects is unpredictable. The opinion involved with weighting parts of a project can't be ignored. While I'm certain that this type of grading is wholly subjective and counterintuitive, teachers who believe in traditional assessment often struggle with the inherent problem illustrated here with Romanoff's Prezi project rubric (Figure 2.1). For his part, Romanoff does see how narrative feedback might replace his rubric, in a place where feedback is perceived as an acceptable means of assessment:

> The Prezi project could be assessed without a score, but there needs to be an environment in which the teacher is willing to evaluate the project without the use of a traditional grading system. Once the instruction has been delivered, and the project assigned and explained, the students get to work. The evaluation should be a discussion. Talking with a student about why their presentation is not visually appealing or needs revision in the writing would cover the first requirement of the rubric. The mathematics could be addressed in the same way. The goal is for students to demonstrate understanding of a topic. Why not tell them what they have done right, and where they need to make corrections?

If Student A and Student B receive this kind of feedback and are given time to make corrections, not only are they likely to complete all parts of the Prezi project, but they can demonstrate mastery learning. Plus, there's no chance of crushing their confidence with a low grade.

TESTS AND NUMBERS

Arguments in favor of grades lose buoyancy when the previous examples are seriously contemplated. If the teacher's opinion plays even the slightest role in assessment, the process becomes alarmingly punitive. Some teachers at the Boston workshop wanted to give Robert a failing grade, based on a difference of opinion about how the conflict writing assignment should be weighted. Similarly, Student A failed the Prezi project because his teacher deemed one part to be worth more than another. Meanwhile, Student B created a carbon copy of Student A's project, yet "earned" a C. The fundamental danger in this kind of assessment is undeniable. At this point, even loyal advocates of traditional grades usually acquiesce to feedback and conversation as better means of assessment. The most tenacious skeptics, though, turn to tests as their last resort in the debate. "Tests are about scores," they will argue. "If there are 100 problems, and Calvin misses 40, he gets 60/100 and a D. In this case, 2 + 2 still equals 4." But does it have to, or is it possible to assess tests without the numbers and without punishing Calvin with that D?

Education researcher, author, and teacher Gerald Aungst, who specializes in alternative assessment in math, argues that what may seem purely objective is not. Aungst contends, as John Romanoff's Prezi project exemplifies, that the intangibles that teachers bring can, in many cases, negate objectivity. "Even on a test or assignment which has only simple skill-based questions and a few word problems, there can be tremendous variation in how it is graded. Although the answer may be right or wrong without any dispute, there are many ancillary things a teacher can grade on the test, which will result in huge variations between teachers." These ancillary items that Aungst (July 2014) alludes to are rarely considered by teachers when creating and evaluating tests but, as he reveals, they create the kind of "noise" that can hinder assessment. Consider the examples of noise that Aungst provides:

- Showing your work (some teachers take off part credit, some won't give any credit for a right answer without any work, some don't care)
- Labeling your answer (some teachers take off a point if a label is missing or wrong, some say the entire answer is wrong if the label is wrong)

- Calculation errors (in some cases, if a student makes a simple computation mistake which results in a wrong answer to a longer problem, the teacher will take off a point or give partial credit, in other cases, the student gets no credit at all)
- Neatness (believe it or not, I've seen teachers who take points off if work is written sloppily, even if it is all correct)

Like the opinion issues in the conflict writing and Prezi project examples, tests also have an array of problems related to subjectivity. Says Aungst, "In the end, the weighting of the various components is usually pretty arbitrary." So, it seems that 2 + 2 doesn't always equal 4.

REFLECTION

How does subjectivity enter into assessment?

With a small group of peers, review a student's assignment. Separately, decide on a grade, based on the teacher's guidelines. Then reconvene and discuss how you decided on the grade.

Next, break away from the group once again and review the same assignment. Supply detailed narrative feedback this time, without a grade (use the SE2R model described in Chapter 3). Then reconvene and compare your feedback with others in the group. What similarities and differences exist? How will the absence of a grade impact learning? Do you find it difficult to supply objective narrative feedback?

Chapter 3 demonstrates how four words can simplify the feedback process.

SE2R—A
Formula for
Change

The only sense that is common in the long run is the
sense of change and we all instinctively avoid it.

—E. B. White, American writer

Mikayla may appear to be an unusual teenager. A student of mine in 2010, Mikayla was not unlike many of her peers, who eagerly accepted narrative feedback about their activities and projects, in lieu of traditional grades. "I always thought feedback would help me more than grades would. I would get a test back with a percentage, but I never knew what I was doing wrong. There would be circles and X's all over my paper that I couldn't make sense of. It all seemed like a big tic-tac-toe game to me. Teachers never left comments. They just expected me to know why something was circled" (Barnes,

2013, p. 68). While perhaps not as outspoken as she, most students are like Mikayla; they long for specific information about their learning. They quietly yearn to talk about what they've done with their peers and their teachers. While they may celebrate high scores on papers and shout hooray over A's on report cards, any student will eagerly submit to more detail about that 90/100 score on a science report. Feedback empowers students to react, while numbers and letters provide a final judgment. After more than a decade of judging my students, I decided to try something new.

REBUILDING ASSESSMENT

Before its final publication, this book had numerous potential titles. Several versions contained the word *formula*. Because of its many negative connotations for educators, who face new formulas for success every year, the word was scrubbed from the final title. Still, SE2R can be described as a formula, but there is nothing negative about it. After studying the extensive research of experts like Dylan Wiliam (2011), Thomas Guskey (2011), Alfie Kohn (2011), and John Hattie (2007), I knew that replacing grades with narrative feedback would be a central piece of transitioning from a traditional to a student-centered classroom, but I also recognized the need to design something that would make providing feedback effective for both my students and for me.

The research clearly defined feedback and distinguished it from the haphazard comments I'd been giving my students for so many years. "The term *feedback* is often used to describe all kinds of comments made after the fact, including advice, praise, and evaluation. But none of these are feedback, strictly speaking" (Wiggins, 2012). Back in my grading days, I routinely scribbled random scores, like 60/75, on students' essays, accompanied by annotations such as these: *awkward, smart, weak, nonsensical, yes, no.* I rarely praised the work or gave advice; praise would have been ineffective but an improvement over my standard comments, which were as irrelevant to learning as the scores I gave the work that were based primarily on instinct or feeling. In my traditional teaching days, there was never the authentic feedback that Grant Wiggins (2012) defines as "goal-referenced; tangible and transparent; actionable; user-friendly (specific and personalized); timely; ongoing; and consistent."

When I came to understand genuine narrative feedback, I felt enlightened. Teaching and learning had new meaning. Still, there had to be assessment. My students had only ever known numbers and letters and meaningless commentary, but I was ready to make learning a conversation. But what about grades? It was inconceivable that the student-centered classroom I'd created could exist with numbers and letters, but learners needed something tangible to replace them. Feeling a little bit like Dr. Frankenstein, I began breaking down everything I had learned in one research-laden summer about narrative feedback and formative assessment and attempted to concoct something new. This wealth of information from an array of sources would eventually morph into an assessment tool that maintained the integrity of valid feedback.

As the school year progressed, I was writing thousands of words of feedback weekly. Much of my free time, a misnomer in education, was spent reviewing the feedback, manipulating it, and determining how to improve it. Too often, those old phrases trickled in. Comments like, "good job," "confusing," and "poorly written" subverted the more objective observations about the work. *What should I write or say that explains what was done and gives students a chance to improve, if their work doesn't demonstrate understanding?* I wondered one evening, while reading my students' essays. What followed was one of those rare *aha* moments. Nothing I'd ever thought of related to academics was so simple, yet so powerful. Contemplating how to improve my feedback and how to obliterate everything subjective helped me come up with the four simple words that directed my narrative feedback from that day forward. Those words are *summarize, explain, redirect,* and *resubmit.*

SE2R: An Overview

Summarize: Provide a one or two sentence summary of what students have accomplished on an activity or project.

Explain: Share detailed observations of what skills or concepts have been mastered based on the specific activity guidelines.

Redirect: Indicate for students the lessons, presentations, or models that need to be reviewed in order to achieve understanding of concepts and mastery of skills.

Resubmit: Encourage students to rework activities, after revisiting prior learning, and resubmit them for further feedback.

This formula removed the subjectivity that had previously undermined legitimate assessment. Instead of telling students what they did right or wrong, what was good or bad, I began sharing observations about what they accomplished, based on lessons and models. To fully understand how SE2R works, consider the following assignment and the feedback that a student might receive.

Class Assignment

1. Write a 400–450-word blog post comparing a character from a novel you've read to an actor's portrayal of that character in a movie version. This can be any novel, as long as there is a movie adaptation.

2. Write two examples of how the actor's portrayal makes the character in the movie appear similar to the character in the novel. Supply details that support your response.

3. Write two examples of how the actor's portrayal makes the character in the movie appear different from the

novel character. Supply details that support your response.

4. Explain, in your opinion, why the actor is a good or bad choice to portray the character.

5. Correctly use two vocabulary words from *List 15* in your blog post. Highlight the words in the color of your choice so your readers can easily locate them.

SUMMARIZE

Students are rarely in tune with precisely what they have accomplished when completing complex tasks. A brief one- or two-sentence summary of what the student accomplished is a critical beginning of effective narrative feedback. This is the *S* in the SE2R model. Without a summary statement, further observations about the work can be blurry or even meaningless. Sometimes, we'd have a one-day assignment or a project checkpoint and I would say, "Tell me what you've done." This direction might be met with a shoulder shrug or a long pause accompanied by wandering eyes, as the student searched for what presumably should be a simple answer. For a blog post comparing a character in a novel to an adaptation of that character in a movie, a student might say, "Uh, I wrote about Katniss and *The Hunger Games*." While this may be generally accurate, a better summary statement written by the teacher as part of the SE2R formula would look like this:

> *You wrote a 400-word blog post comparing the character Katniss Everdeen from the novel* The Hunger Games *to the character as portrayed by Jennifer Lawrence in the movie version.*

This one-sentence summary specifically defines what the student accomplished, anchoring the remaining feedback to this particular activity. This summary is especially important when feedback is provided on a platform that is separate from the student's work. For example, if the SE2R for the blog post were left on a web-based grade book, a student might easily link the comments to a different activity, if the summary statement were omitted.

EXPLAIN

The problem with explaining a student's achievement on a task is that the explanation often leads to judgment rather than observation about any existing gaps between instruction and learning. "A major aim of the educative process is to assist in identifying these gaps ("How am I going?" relative to "Where am I going?") and to provide remediation in the form of alternative or other steps ("Where to next?")" (Hattie & Timperly, 2007, p. 102). As stated previously, when I originally eliminated grades, the feedback I wrote was plagued by subjectivity. Frustrated with this poor assessment practice, I returned to the researchers who had originally inspired my affinity for a no-grades classroom. Hattie, Kohn, Wiggins and others reminded me that it is far more important to indicate how and where a student was going based on prior learning and on the guidelines of an activity, than it is to give that student an opinion. Telling Emily that a sentence in her essay is "loosely constructed" had no bearing on what she'd learned about writing coherent prose. The key to the explanation is to make observations, based solely on an assignment's specific guidelines. Writing clear assignment guidelines and supplying detailed instructions is a critical subtext, as the SE2R is always tied to these guidelines.

Assume that the student writing about *The Hunger Games* identifies two similarities (item 2 in the assignment guidelines), properly uses two vocabulary words (item 4), shares an opinion about the choice of actors (item 5), but does not provide examples of differences in the novel character and the actor's portrayal (item 3 in the assignment guidelines). We know, based on the summary statement, that the blog post contains at least 400 words. One piece of the assignment is missing. So, for the Explain portion of this student's SE2R feedback, the teacher would write or say something like this:

You clearly identified two similarities between Katniss from the novel and the actor who portrayed Katniss in the movie, and you properly use the words, savagery *and* eviscerate *in your narrative. You've also provided an opinion of why the actor is a good choice. I didn't notice any identified differences in your post, though. Did you see any? This was item 3 on the guidelines.*

In the grade world, the author of this blog post is likely to receive a poor score because a significant portion of the assignment is incomplete—20 percent, if the grader weights each section equally (recall the issues shared in Chapter 2 with weighting assignments). In a classroom founded on conversation and narrative feedback, the student can still demonstrate mastery learning without the teacher's opinion and a punitive grade impeding the process. Notice the polite observation and the question in the feedback. These set a positive tone because they are unbiased. Students respond well to objective observations like "I didn't see this" and questions like "Can you do this?" or "Did I overlook it?" This kind of feedback stimulates a conversation about learning, even if the feedback is written. (See Appendix C for more examples of objective feedback to use in your class.) When SE2R is supplied digitally, students will often answer questions or respond to observations. Sometimes, their response is as simple as "I went to my locker, and I forgot to finish the post." A cornucopia of issues outside of school can interfere with learning, and traditional measurements are incapable of factoring in these issues.

REDIRECT AND RESUBMIT

This book contains many examples of how an environment built on meaningful feedback is enriching for both teachers and students. The best part of SE2R and something that is too often absent from classrooms around the world is the opportunity for students to return to prior learning, change an activity, and resubmit it for further feedback. Because teachers are driven by standards, pacing charts, and a frantic race to prepare students for standardized tests, there appears to be little time to pause and allow struggling students to revisit the lessons and models that connect to assignments and projects. There's even less time for students to modify work and give it back to the teacher for further review. Slowing down the instructional process, though, is vital to learning, and ignoring this necessary slowdown deprives students of the opportunity to master concepts and skills. This is even more devastating when knowledge required for future learning is lost, because the teacher is racing to check off an objective on a pacing chart.

The author of the character blog post failed to complete one of the five parts of the assignment. This omission was observed in the Explain portion of the SE2R. (See Figure 3.1 for all of the SE2R feedback provided on the blog post assignment.)

| **Figure 3.1** Sample SE2R for Blog Post Assignment |

Summarize: You wrote a 400-word blog post comparing the character Katniss Everdeen from the novel *The Hunger Games* to the character as portrayed by Jennifer Lawrence in the movie version.

Explain: You clearly identified two similarities between Katniss from the novel and the actor who portrayed Katniss in the movie, and you properly use the words *savagery* and *eviscerate* in your narrative. You've also provided an opinion of why the actor is a good choice. I didn't notice any identified differences in your post, though. Did you see any? This was item 3 on the guidelines.

Redirect: Please return to the post and identify two differences between Katniss in the novel and Katniss as she is portrayed in the movie. Be sure to provide details that support these differences.

Resubmit: When you finish, let me know that you've made changes to the blog post.

In a traditional points model, the student would likely receive a grade of C or D on the blog post, depending on a wide range of variables. In a class that focuses only on mastery learning, the student is redirected and asked to resubmit in this manner:

Please return to the post and identify two differences between Katniss in the novel and Katniss as she is portrayed in the movie. Be sure to provide details that support these differences. When you finish, let me know that you've made changes to the blog post.

A critical distinction between grades and Assessment 3.0, using the SE2R formula or something similar, is how feedback encourages learning, while grades negate it. Give this student a D on her blog post and she may grow to dislike writing in general and novel evaluation in particular, as she'll equate these to a bad experience—an aversion similar to a person disdaining a once-favorite food after becoming sick from it. The naysayer contends that allowing students to return to completed activities encourages negligence or laziness. Not only is there little research to support this claim, laziness in most cases will have played no role at all. The student may have simply forgotten to complete a part of the guidelines. This is fallibility, not negligence. Given the opportunity to return to the work, the student, in most cases, will perfect it. There are rare cases when students elect to move on to something new, because they feel they can illustrate what they have learned in a fresh activity or project. This is always fine because students embrace SE2R when given the choice to make changes or to progress to something new. The result of this simple approach to assessment is the creation of enthusiastic independent learners: Students who are eager to complete activities and projects— not because they desire a high grade but because they feel enriched by the knowledge they acquire and by the result of their work.

SE2R in High School

An educator once told me that replacing grades with SE2R feedback is easy for elementary and middle school teachers. After all, grades don't really matter until you get to high school, when GPAs count for college admission. It's hard to argue that GPAs have more value in high school than they do in the primary and middle levels—an interesting irony, considering that this book is about eliminating grades. If in the current education climate grades do indeed impact a student after middle school, it's important to examine whether a no-grades, feedback-only assessment system can function effectively in high school, thus eliminating the need for a GPA. Is it plausible for Assessment 3.0 to work at a competitive high school with challenging Advanced Placement (AP) and International Baccalaureate (IB) courses? Veteran teacher and administrator Charles Gleek grappled with this issue for years before making his own transition to an assessment system based on narrative feedback and student self-evaluation.

A high school teacher and IB Global Politics curriculum and assessment developer at Broward Prep in Florida, Gleek considered a variety of factors before initiating the use of SE2R in his classes. "I don't think there was a particular incident that made me think, ok, enough of this grading craziness," says Gleek (July 2014). "If I were to sum it up in a single idea, my move to reject traditional grading occurred when I decided that engagement and conversation were to be the centerpieces of my teaching philosophy. When you spend time actually getting to know the students in your classes, you come to the realization that their diversity of interests, of expertise, and of skill sets do not all fit into a nice little set of boxes labeled A's, B's, C's, etc." Interested in altering his methods, Gleek sought inspiration and insight from people outside of his school. Twitter became another powerful resource, as Gleek collaborated with parents and other education professionals in ongoing conversations in cyberspace. These discussions about best practices were, according to

Gleek, essential to moving away from traditional grading to narrative feedback. "I had the opportunity to bounce ideas off other teachers and learn from the successes and failures they were kind enough to share with everyone."

During his time as an assistant principal, Gleek participated in parent conferences that all too often were focused on grades. Conditioned to concentrate on individual assignment scores and how they impacted an overall grade, some parents confronted Gleek about teachers who deprived their children of what sometimes turned out to be a fraction of a percentage point. "For me, the dichotomy couldn't be more apparent. Students and parents and teachers were always interested in having conversations about learning, but it was the notion of grades, the rigidity of 100-point scales or 5-point rubrics that always got in the way. The feedback I received and information I learned from these conversations as an administrator encouraged me to continue and expand the pedagogy of conversation in the classes that I teach." Not long after these encounters and his contemplation of the assessment practices he was using, Gleek transitioned his classroom to narrative feedback, including SE2R. "I found that having a conversation with each and every student about their work—from essays to projects to even designing traditional summative examinations—generated more engagement in what we were learning, yielded better results on the assessments themselves, and led to a more substantive understanding of the course objectives or standards."

As you'll see in Chapter 4, middle school students like Christina and Tori, in classes built on SE2R feedback, overcome personal issues that interfere with learning, often exceeding even the highest expectations. Charles Gleek has experienced similar success at the high school level. Class discussions are not limited to individual assignments and projects; conversations about feedback have helped students flesh out how they learn. Eleventh-grader Carissa DeRanek is one of many students in Gleek's classes who rave about the influence of SE2R feedback.

So far, I really appreciate the fact that we have feedback instead of a grade. I found last year that having specific feedback was really helpful in figuring out when I was or wasn't headed in the right direction. Last year, [my teacher] was great about going over all of my essays with me because social studies essays have always been a little daunting to me. However, I like that my essays aren't graded at all this year because it makes it feel like less of a scary exercise and more like sharing my thoughts and getting suggestions about new ways to look at and analyze things (DeRanek, 2013, personal correspondence; used with permission).

Like most schools, even those moving away from traditional grades in the classroom, Broward Prep still issues report cards. Gleek and his students refuse to submit entirely to a practice that opposes the assessment model they've grown accustomed to using in class every day, opting instead to have students assign grades themselves. When others hear about self-grading, Gleek (July 2014) says, they become intrigued by the entire process:

One of the most frequent conversation topics I have with colleagues, parents, as well as students who are interested in taking IB Global Politics begins with something like this, "I heard that you don't give grades in your class; how do you do that?" Of course, I explain that the students and I decide their grades each term. These grades are the result of each student's and my professional, shared reflection on the work we have done each term. Throughout each year, students read hundreds of pages of text from primary and secondary sources, including policy and academic journals. Students watch and analyze days of documentary footage and expert analysis. They research complex topics and phenomena, participate in diplomatic and crisis games and simulations nearly every week. They write analytical summaries of the literature they encounter;

develop, research, and communicate their own research through papers and presentations; and reflect thoughtfully on their experience through regular debriefings, surveys, and conversations with me. In short, the extent to which a student approaches, meets, or exceeds the expectations of our prescribed learning outcomes is a function of each individual student's and my shared perception. I have found that the students and I are keenly aware of their own intellectual strengths, as well as areas in which they should improve.

Students from schools like Broward Prep are characteristically competitive about grades. They are preparing for challenging colleges and high-paying jobs, and they have spent much of their academic lives doing everything within their reach to earn high grades. Yet, Gleek's IB students have disdained all forms of measurement, embracing SE2R feedback and conversation about learning. It's reasonable to speculate that if students in this high-pressure private-school environment can willingly abandon everything they've ever known about grades, students in any school can follow their lead—whether that school is an elementary, middle, or even a high school.

REFLECTION

How do you envision SE2R in your own classroom or school?

Consider replacing traditional grades with SE2R feedback for one assignment, project, or unit. Many teachers who have completely disdained grades started their transition this way.

Chapter 7 gives specific tips on how to effectively replace grades with narrative feedback, creating a culture of self-evaluative independent learners.

Coppell Middle School East

The visionary starts with a clean sheet of paper, and re-imagines the world.

—Malcolm Gladwell, *New York Times* bestselling author

I n the summer of 2013, Laura Springer made a decision that many educators might call crazy. Principal of Coppell Independent School District's East Middle School, nestled in a quiet little suburb in Dallas County (Texas), Springer wanted something revolutionary for her students. So, after her own summer of reading and reflecting, Springer attempted something that had never been done in the Lone Star state—turning some of her classes into Results Only Learning Environments (ROLE). "Results-only learning is a system that eliminates most methods teachers currently use. It involves embracing the final result of learning rather than focusing on traditional practices, such as homework, worksheets, tests, and grades" (Barnes,

2013, p. 7). Realizing that results-only learning questions established norms, Springer decided to ease her school into it, so she asked several teachers to be part of a pilot team. They would throw out everything they'd ever done that might be called "in-the-box" teaching, including most notably traditional grades.

THE PILOT TEAM

Kat Julian was one of the traditional teachers recruited by Springer. "Throwing out everything I ever knew about teaching was the scariest thing I have ever done in my career," Julian told me when we discussed her work on the pilot team a year later. After 100 percent of her 8th graders passed the Texas standardized reading test, Julian called her new classroom a masterpiece. "I walked away from this scary year with 105 young adults that I know have the will and the know-how to change this world we live in."

Laura Melson, another teacher on Coppell East's pilot team, had a similar experience. She says, "I really wanted to focus more on learners' improvements, progress, and personal achievements rather than grades. Grade conferences made that possible. We focused on specific reading and writing skills each marking period, and in grade conferences I was able to truly see what was mastered." Julian, Melson, and Megan Boyd, the third member of the pilot team, demonstrate the unique power that SE2R brings to assessment—the capacity to reveal a new understanding of learning for students.

A DIFFICULT TRANSITION

Despite the simplicity built into the SE2R model, the transition from traditional grading is challenging. Hadley Ferguson, a teacher in Philadelphia and a Library of Congress advisory board member, also moved her middle school classroom to a system built on feedback. Ferguson (2013) explains the challenges of eliminating grades this way: "Teaching outside the security of a system of grades that everyone understood was initially intimidating. Classrooms with grades were a familiar shore that everyone knew" (p. 195). Coppell East's Melson bears out Ferguson's assertion. "This remarkable transformation away from grades to the SE2R system was not easy. I wasn't sure how I was going to implement this initially, but through collaboration and planning, I finally found a groove." One of the issues teachers face when using SE2R or similar kinds of narrative feedback is encouraging students to buy in. Because most students have seen nothing but numbers and letters on activities throughout their academic lives, the change to feedback can come as a shock. "At first, it was confusing for my sixth-grade bunch because they were so used to grades," says Melson, "but as the year progressed, especially the second semester, they understood and focused on improving their reading and writing skills. They wanted to master skills and they wanted to show off their new skills! It was remarkable to see the significant change in their reading and, especially, their writing, while taking away traditional grades."

CHRISTINA

Christina read much more slowly than her peers. Her teacher, Megan Boyd, encouraged her language arts students to read daily, which was a daunting task for Christina, who hadn't read many books in her life. In the grade world, in which she'd lived for her entire school career prior to 7th Grade, Christina might settle for a C in language arts, especially a class in which the teacher was challenging students to read dozens of books in one year. However, this was a much different school year Christina quickly learned.

> The best part was not seeing her self-evaluation become more positive. It was seeing her self-confidence soar.
>
> —Megan Boyd, East Middle School teacher

She watched her peers devour books, while she trudged through struggling to keep their pace. Meanwhile, Boyd provided specific feedback about Christina's reading habits and strategies, and the two conversed about how Christina learned. These conversations and the omission of punitive grades emboldened Christina. With encouragement from her teacher, the absence of pressure, and the freedom to choose books that interested her, Christina's reading rate improved. Coppell East operates on six-week reporting periods, so the pilot team was forced to supply report card grades, whether the teachers wanted to or not. In a class built on narrative feedback and self-evaluation, Christina's final grade improved in each marking period. A steady increase in her reading rate, coupled with careful reflection on the SE2R feedback Boyd was providing, helped Christina's writing progress dramatically. Boyd summarizes Christina's story this way: "The best part was not seeing her self-evaluation become more positive. It was seeing her self-confidence soar. By the end of the year, she had much more confidence and passion about her learning and had read more books than ever before."

ASSESSMENT WITHOUT COMPARISON

Christina read 25 books that year, an astonishing number considering that she had difficulty reading throughout elementary school. Her peers read roughly 10 more books on average. In a classroom that is built on measuring learning with numbers and percentages, Christina might have still been a C student; after all, she read nearly 30 percent less than her peers in a class where reading is the quintessential skill. Some might even call her a failure. With the subjectivity that accompanies grades, it's easy to manipulate the numbers to label Christina's performance anything from good to average to poor. But if we remove the numbers, the percentages, and the grades from assessment, the subjectivity also disappears. Christina's teacher explains it best:

Feedback places students in a category all their own. This girl's accomplishments were truly huge accomplishments if you only compare her performance to her ability. If you were to compare her performance with another student's, she may look, once again, as just a mediocre, slow-processing reader. It isn't fair, though, to compare her or belittle her progress, success, or accomplishments with another learner's. She deserves the right to grow, process, and succeed at a rate that works for her and then celebrate when she meets her goals! That's what feedback has the power to produce in a classroom. (2014)

TORI

Before entering Laura Melson's sixth-grade language arts class, Tori was a bit of an enigma. She excelled in a variety of academic areas. In fact, she was in the Gifted-Talented program in elementary school. In spite of her obvious intelligence and creativity, Tori was not a good writer. She is dyslexic, which puts even the most enthusiastic readers and writers at a disadvantage. After years of poor results (she failed the Texas state writing test in fourth grade), Tori was placed in remediation. This was devastating for a child with her skills, one who enjoys sewing and designing clothes and accessories. "In fifth grade, she told me she was at the stupid table, meaning the low group," says Tori's mom, Susan Hall, recalling her daughter's rough elementary years. "She asked if she could be home schooled or skip to college."

Despite her dyslexia and weak language arts skills, Tori had excelled enough in other areas that she set her sights on Pre-AP (advanced placement) language arts at East Middle School. Principal Springer spoke to Tori's parents about the ROLE pilot program and convinced them to put Tori in Melson's class. For her part, Melson assured Tori that she would be challenged as much in the ROLE as she would in the Pre-AP class. Melson explained that in a results-only classroom, students work at the pace that is best for them. Tori would have the freedom to learn without the pressure of receiving failing grades, even if she struggled with a heavy reading load. The results-only classroom was the perfect environment for Tori, who took on the advanced class challenge of reading 25 books, even though she wasn't required to do so. As the calendar pages turned, Tori read daily and she wrote constantly. More important, she pored over Melson's SE2R feedback and conversed with her teacher frequently about her writing. "Tori challenged herself in her writing by consistently reviewing feedback and asking questions about how to make her writing better," Melson explains. "Throughout the school year, I tried to give her the opportunity to be creative and imaginative in her writing since those were her strengths." Tori was growing into a self-critical, graceful writer, who responded to feedback by challenging herself to improve.

Susan Hall marveled at her daughter's progress. "The growth I saw in the work Tori was producing was nothing but amazing. She went from a few unorganized sentences with little imagery and proper use of punctuation to stories you enjoyed reading."

Hall is a teacher, so her assessment is more critical than what most doting mothers might supply. Nothing validates her evaluation more than Tori's writing. This is an excerpt from a fictional piece Tori wrote after months of feedback and coaching from Melson—minus any punitive grades, of course.

"See you at 7:00," I told my mom as she dropped me off at dance. As I walked into the studio I heard pointe music playing in the background. I went to put my gold sparkling dance bag on my hook in the small pink hall with other dance bags that line the wall. I took an envelope out of my bag containing the tuition. I dropped it in the mailbox by the dance hall noticing how the rough edges of the paper glided across the metal box. After taking care of business I walked into the dance room and put on my tap shoes, "clack, bam, crash." We stomped, kicked and scurried across the floor to the rhythm of the tap music,

Tori responds to SE2R feedback.

making all kinds of noises. The salty stench of sweat ran across the room like we were dancing in a football locker room. At last, class was finally over. "Phew" I sighed in relief. (Tori Hall, 6th grade student, East Middle School)

Teachers are rarely willing to take credit for their students' successes. Laura Melson is no different. "I mainly gave her the voice and choice of her reading and writing," Melson says about Tori's transformation from a confused and disgruntled elementary student who couldn't pass a simple standardized writing test to a promising young writer. "I let her write what she wanted, how she wanted, and throughout the year, we built upon writing techniques. She took these techniques and made them her own."

And never once did Tori or her parents ask about a grade on her writing. "More importantly, to me as a parent, was the confidence she gained in herself," Tori's mother says. "Tori and I talked a lot this year about the difference between the ROLE classes and her regular classes. One of many comments she made was 'I am free to be me.' I asked her what that meant and she said she could do her work to make it better without being scared of a bad grade because she did not get it right the first time. That is powerful."

Improving Feedback, Increasing Achievement

As the school year passed, the Coppell East teachers honed their SE2R feedback, and students, most with unique stories like Christina's and Tori's, used the feedback to improve and become independent learners. What the pilot team didn't realize was that the more feedback they provided, the more proof of learning they created, eliminating the need for multiple choice tests and other summative assessments. In effect, they were creating SE2R portfolios, which will be examined more in Chapter 5. Although feedback could be written on paper or be given during conversations, the teachers delivered much of it electronically. For example, in Figure 4.1, a complete SE2R comment is left on a student's essay in a Google document.

The teacher briefly summarizes the activity, explains what is covered in the writing and what is missing, and includes redirection and a request for resubmission. When students return to the work and improve it, based on the feedback, the next comment leaves off the 2R portion of the SE2R. Figure 4.2 illustrates this. The teacher explains exactly what has been learned in a list and makes it clear that the student has mastered the concepts: "After 3 submissions," she writes, "you nailed this."

This ongoing online conversation about learning inspires students to constantly improve an activity over time. Since the student in Figure 4.2 submitted the essay three times, some lessons must have been missed in the original versions. The two iterations after redirection from the teacher provide the extra opportunity the student needs to perfect the skills and demonstrate mastery. If Kat Julian used assessment 2.0, she could have arbitrarily assigned 100 points to the essay. The student might

Figure 4.1 SE2R Comment

V. To overcome this we have to teach the dangers and effects drugs can do to se after teens take the one drug, their life has already collapsed. The goal is to and prevent teens dealing with the drug abuse or preventing future teens to do

ther *belief* I have is teens being able to find activities that they are interested in to eep their minds off of the substances. This can help them because instead of re and more drugs they can find something that will interest them. It is important ests because during a drug addiction they will be depressed and push their family I did some research, the emotional period affects loved ones too. In a video I Woman that was telling her story of how she didn't want anybody around her and Wanted to do was to curl up in a ball and cry. There was another woman who said ed her mother by not ever sleeping, losing her job, and dad having two heart to stress and trying to find her on the streets. I have not witnessed people dealing because I choose the right friends and live in a great environment.

ongly *believe* what should happen is getting the teen's parents involved. I s because sometimes the parents do not know what's happening in their own r who they are friends with, as they get older. Once teens get hooked on drugs will be going down hill until they die since the symptoms do not go away. They will ecover from the bad choices they have encountered. The parents can get involved who they hang out with, talking with them, etc. Therefore, their parents can make

Kat Julian 9:34 AM Apr 24
As i read I see a lot of our dead words used…remember these do not capture the reader's attention. You have strong arguments, so let's make sure people hear your belief and passion. Please make the changes and mark resolved. Resubmit by Friday.
vmd6408 9:30 PM Apr 24
Marked as resolved
Kat Julian 10:27 AM Jun 20
Re-opened

Figure 4.2   Comment Without 2R

* A cold, sharp, razor touching soft, pale skin, the razor slices through, as blood pools around like a volcano slowly erupting. I keep going deeper and deeper, as relief washes over me, as if I am no longer drowning. ***Self Harm.** sounds like someone's trying to get attention, right?
Not really. some of these people are getting bullied, abused, or just really stressed. **They** cut to release whatever they're feeling inside, and what can't be explained in word. **Cutting** may give them maybe a few minutes of pleasure, but *I believe that this pleasure doesn't last very long. *I believe this pleasure, could possibly be the last time they feel good about themselves.
*I believe we can all end self harming, one step at a time.

* Just like every problem there is a solution. There are other ways to release all this hatred.
* All this anger and all these feelings that have been eating you up, on the inside. Being able to talk to someone, like a counselor, family friend, or just anyone you really trust, will allowed you to express your self. You will be able to connect with other people with the same problems.

Next, writing your problems out would be almost like talking to someone. **You're** *pouring your heart out into your writing, because being able to express yourself is a great feeling, just like being in control. **Writing** may not work for everybody, but there are other ways to deal with self harm.

Likewise, punching something, running or just simply working out, can help ease your anger. **Being** able to put your anger into what you're doing, will be one of the easiest ways to let go of all your built up negative emotions. **Working** out is also a distraction, to prevention of self harming. **Using** these solutions,

Kat Julian
10:30 AM Today

You have mastered our writing standards for this task! Strong Word Choice Argument and Supports Fallacies and Rhetorical Devices Strong conclusion So very proud of all your hard work. After 3 resubmissions, you nailed this!

have scored 50 points after one attempt and received an F. Instead of learning, the student might feel like a failure, and this could have impacted future effort and, in turn, performance. Based on her experience in her own no-grades classroom, Hadley Ferguson (2013) agrees:

> An A means you are safe and smart, and an F means your work and, by association, you have been judged a failure. Letting go of that system and creating a new one forced the members of the education community to change and grow. In an ungraded classroom, the role of the teacher is the first one to shift. I was moving away from seeing my role as being the single authority in the room, the person who knew what good work looked like and passed judgment based on my knowledge and experience.... My goal was more than to impart history content to each student; it was to create an independent learner. (p. 195)

Independent learners are successful students. They take lessons and models from class and turn them into skills. Independent learners read on their own time, use the Internet for research, and manage content efficiently on social media. Although I would argue that standardized testing is a poor assessment of learning, independent learners, who have cultivated their skills in no-grades, narrative feedback classrooms, typically perform well on high stakes tests. There is a dearth of empirical data as to why this is, but there are plenty of examples of this success.

THE NUMBERS THAT MATTER

When I first created a Results Only Learning Environment, I was coming off a year in which less than 70 percent of my students passed Ohio's state-mandated achievement test. That year, many days a month were consumed by test manipulation strategies and practice achievement tests. In the ROLE, test practice was banished, along with all other traditional teaching methods. Instead students selected projects to work on throughout the school year. We read daily, wrote constantly, and conversed about learning. Although I didn't need standardized tests to know my students were learning, the passing rate increased more than 20 percent, when traditional practices and grades were eliminated.

When I visited Coppell to discuss their move to results-only learning and no-grades classrooms, Julian, Melson, and Boyd expressed concern about their own forthcoming standardized tests. Unlike some schools, who were battling low reading and writing scores, Coppell East's test results had been more than acceptable, and the pilot team teachers believed that if their students posted low scores, the ROLE experiment would be highly scrutinized and possibly even abolished. Nine months later, their fears vanished. When the test results came back, 97 percent of the pilot team's 327 students passed the Texas STAAR reading test. Most notable was that 58 percent of Coppell East's eighth graders scored in the advanced range, while 88 percent of Julian's students were advanced. It may seem like a contradiction for me to tout these statistics in the same space in which I espouse the elimination of numbers and percentages. This point can't be underestimated, though. In an education system that values standardized testing as its most treasured means for assessing learning, many observers believe that a student-centered classroom that eliminates all form of measurement and disdains test preparation and practice will contain students who perform poorly on tests. As noted earlier, this kind of environment breeds independent learners, who develop the kind of confidence that the average student in a traditional classroom doesn't typically have.

> This is a system that hits at the heart of why we became educators in the first place.
>
> —Laura Springer, principal, East Middle School

Coppell East students are reading more than ever, producing amazing yearlong projects, reacting to SE2R feedback that they receive online and via individual conversations with teachers, and turning into independent learners, who score at amazingly high rates on standardized tests. Based on these results and overwhelming support from parents, administrators have plans to delve even deeper into student-centered learning and no-grades classrooms in the future. Neighboring school administrators have sent representatives to East Middle School to explore the revolutionary methods of the pilot team, and plans are in place for their own transformation.

Photo by Laura Melson.

Coppell girls review narrative feedback.

Principal Laura Springer (2014), who ignited the change, summarizes the impact of East's transition from traditional to progressive, no-grades classrooms.

To leave a system behind that just assigns numerical grading to a student, as opposed to a growth system that promotes learning, has been life changing. My parents, students, and teachers have been reinvigorated about what true learning brings to each student. We have seen such growth in our writing and reading from our students. Parents have been so overwhelmed with the Results Only Learning Environment. It is a change that we will continue to use as it allows us to facilitate risk taking and challenges. We are sold on this program and the feedback piece of the system is where we have seen the most growth. Our educators are improving as teachers as they pinpoint learners' needs and provide them pathways to growth through consistent feedback. Our students are begging to get into the ROLE classrooms so that they can be active participants in the learning process. We can step away from the testing environment and standardized world to be able to really teach our learners with a growth model. This is a system that hits at the heart of why we became educators in the first place.

REFLECTION

- Do you have a Christina or Tori in your class or school? How do you think that student might respond to SE2R feedback?
- Which step in the SE2R process do you feel will be most challenging for you? For your students?
- What do you envision parents saying to a class built on SE2R feedback?
- How might you and your colleagues deal with pushback from parents and other education shareholders?

Involving Students

Tell me and I forget. Teach me and I remember. Involve me and I learn.

—Benjamin Franklin, author,
inventor, U.S. Founding Father

Throughout her entire school life, Jasmine understood one kind of assessment—number and letter grades. Every paper she had ever written, every project, and every quiz was returned with an arbitrary number or percentage, which translated to a corresponding A through F letter grade. An enthusiastic student, Jasmine sat at an old table with a laptop computer perched obtrusively in front of her. She typed as feverishly as her unskilled fingers would allow, and a summary of the book she read the past summer gradually came to life on a web page that her teacher built for her. "I like the detail you give about the protagonist." My voice echoed from behind Jasmine, startling the young author, who turned sheepishly and whispered, "What's it worth?"

After a moment of contemplation, I shrugged and answered her question with one of my own: "What do *you* think it's worth?"

Visibly confused, Jasmine pursed her lips and studied her shoes before answering my question with two more of her own: "I mean how many points is it? What grade do you think it will get?"

I sat in the open chair next to her. "Let's discuss it. Tell me what you have done and what you've learned from the assignment. If we absolutely had to put a grade on it, how would *you* grade it?"

Jasmine's eyebrows furrowed, her lips tightened again, and her shoulders shrugged. Then, her head nodded from right to left. "I don't know."

"You have to know," I said, my chin resting on clasped fingers. "Because your opinion is what matters most."

At that moment, everything Jasmine had ever learned about assessment was changing. She would never receive a number or letter, she learned, on anything she produced in her language arts class from that point forward. Jasmine and her peers, and most students around the world, had been victims of assessment 2.0 for their entire school lives. Anything different from a measurement was foreign to them. "What if I don't think it's very good?" Jasmine asked. "Will I get an F?"

I slowly rose pushed in the chair, patted the eager author on her shoulder and smiled. "Just keep writing, Jasmine. It's already better than you know."

> By removing letter grades from the final product, it ceased being exactly that, final.
>
> —Pernille Ripp (2014), teacher and education author

Old-school assessment practices are not only detrimental to learning for many reasons, including the ones outlined in Chapter 1, they leave students out of the process, which is both illogical and sad. "Grades tell students that even though they devour their books and can't wait to talk to somebody about them, when they forget to include the title and author on a book report, they must not be "A+" readers. Grading tells students that they may have way too much responsibility at the age of 10, but that I don't care whether they're too tired today to do their best work" (Ripp, 2014, p. 113). And students do indeed have bad days, often caused by issues unrelated to learning. Let's not forget how Tori, in Chapter 4, struggled with writing in elementary school, due in large part to her dyslexia—a learning disability that her state-mandated standardized test did not consider, when labeling her a failure. Eliminating traditional grades allows students to overcome days when they are not at their best, when peripheral problems interfere with academics. More important, the SE2R (Summarize, Explain, Redirect, Resubmit) process creates learning opportunities that never end. "By removing letter grades from the final product, it ceased being exactly that, final. Now when an assignment is handed in, my students know it may not be done. It is no longer seen as an end product, but instead as another potential stepping stone in our learning journey" (Ripp, 2014, p. 114).

THE DANGER OF TOO MUCH WRITTEN FEEDBACK

Narrative feedback is not simply written descriptors of work. When used in concert with the student, feedback turns into a beautiful conversation about learning. When I first abandoned grades, I was so caught up in providing SE2R feedback that I didn't realize that what I had done was create an ongoing *War and Peace*–type narrative for my students. I was disappointed to learn that much of the feedback I was writing was being overlooked or, in some cases, completely ignored. One day, I returned part of a lengthy project. It was written on paper, as this was prior to the days when I taught in a classroom filled with computers. Weaving my way through the pods of tables where my students sat in small groups, I was shocked to see that many weren't reading the comments that I had spent hours writing. "What did you think of my feedback?" I asked several students. When my query was met with shrugs, I realized something was terribly wrong. Forging ahead, I asked several enthusiastic students, who had mastered this particular activity, why they hadn't read the feedback. "Honestly," a brave boy whispered "you write stuff every day. It can get a bit long."

"Okay," I answered, "so tell me exactly what you did and why you did it." Each student in the group burst into a brief dissertation about his or her project, eager to share near-textbook commentary about their work. This enthusiastic dialogue helped me conclude that the problem wasn't with my precisely written SE2R feedback. It was that the students weren't part of the conversation. It occurred to me at that moment that lengthy written feedback wasn't necessary for every activity or project checkpoint. Sometimes, it is best to ask students a simple question about their work and allow the conversation to soar.

SE2R SHORTHAND

The day students told me that daily written feedback was too much was a revelation. I knew that eliminating grades in favor of SE2R would radically increase my workload, but I was determined to proceed with as much feedback as possible, believing that it was the right thing to do. Once I moved beyond the frustration of knowing that students were ignoring some of my feedback, it struck me that this was a logical and wonderful thing. Now, I could write less and help my students more by creating an ongoing dialogue about learning. Furthermore, I could record any discussions that I believed to be necessary additions to our online grade book, which I used only to provide feedback to students (mainly for report card conferences) and parents. If students were completing a written critique of a peer's novel reflection on their blogs, I might want brief feedback online as a record of this ongoing activity and of our discussions. The blog post commenting helped students learn how to give constructive feedback, while improving their writing skills, which was something we examined not only weekly but also at the end of a marking period when it was time to settle on report card grades. There's more on report cards later in this chapter.

Chats with individuals during blogging could move quickly, and with more than 100 students, forgetting the details of these conversations was easy. Because SE2R was always part of any discussion about academics, another system for annotating this dialogue helped when adding lengthier feedback. I call this system *SE2R shorthand*. Figure 5.1 is an example of SE2R shorthand for the novel reflection critique.

Figure 5.1 SE2R Shorthand

Activity: Reflection Critique	
Note	**SE2R Conversion**
<300	You have completed your critique according to guidelines, but it is less than 300 words. Please lengthen it and resubmit.
>500	You have completed your critique according to guidelines, but it is more than 500 words. Please cut unnecessary portions of the critique and resubmit.
DM	You wrote a 300-500-word critique, with a properly used vocabulary word, but you did not include an example of a key detail that demonstrates understanding of our model critique. Please add a key detail to your post and resubmit.
DU	You wrote a 300-500-word critique, with a properly used vocabulary word, but your example of a key detail that demonstrates understanding of our model critique is unclear. Please explain how the detail you supplied indicates the author's understanding of the model critique and resubmit.
V	You wrote a 300-500-word critique, with an example of a key detail that demonstrates understanding of our model critique, but you left out a properly used, highlighted vocabulary word from our student word bank. Please add a vocabulary word to your post and resubmit.
M	You wrote a 300-500-word critique, with an example of a key detail that demonstrates understanding of our model critique. You included a properly used, highlighted vocabulary word from our student word bank. You have mastered this activity, according to our guidelines. Well done.

The rows represent the types of shorthand notes I wrote on a clipboard that contained my class roster. The roster was printed in a spreadsheet, so blocks appeared next to each student. These had a variety of uses and one was shorthand notes. Guidelines for the novel reflection critiques instructed students to write 300 to 500 words.

One shorthand designation I might add to my clipboard for an individual could indicate that the critique is less than 300 words. I would ask if the student could add any detail to the post, but until it was done, I would write this note next to the student's name: < 300. Students were also instructed to mention one specific detail from the author of the post they were reviewing and explain why it fit our class model of a well-written critique. If the blog post was missing this important portion of the activity, I would mention it during a one-to-one conversation, but I'd also note it on my class roster like this: DM (detail missing). If the interpretation of the author's detail was unclear, I would use this shorthand note: DU (detail unclear). Since vocabulary was a central piece on all writing activities, the guidelines for the novel reflection critique called for at least one properly used, highlighted vocabulary word from the student-generated word bank (a long list of new words we created from books students read as part of our Reading All Year project). If the vocabulary word was omitted from the critique or used improperly or was not highlighted, I would make this shorthand note: V (vocabulary). Of course, in an individual discussion about an assignment it's easy to flesh out a simple problem like this one. In most cases, the problem can be rectified quickly. If it's a simple highlighting matter, this can be taken care of immediately, and a shorthand note isn't necessary. For students who have completed all parts of the activity according to the guidelines, the shorthand designation is M for *mastery*.

YES, YOU HAVE TIME FOR FEEDBACK

At some point in the day, during a planning period or after school, I take the shorthand notes and convert them to SE2R feedback, which is placed in the comment section of the online grade book or directly beneath each student's blog post. Opponents of written narrative feedback, instead of grades, contend that there isn't enough time to write the kinds of narratives shown in this book. "I'd love to give my students SE2R feedback," a teacher told me at a conference once, "but with 120 students, I simply don't have the time." My first response to this argument is that all feedback doesn't have to be written. Often, verbal feedback is enough. However, for teachers who are compelled to have some kind of daily assessment placed in a grade book (some schools mandate this), shorthand SE2R reduces the time significantly, and the amazing benefits are not lost.

Consider the shorthand notes in Figure 5.1, focusing on the detailed narrative conversions. Efficiency dictates setting up shorthand notes and lengthier conversions before assessing an activity. This can be done for just about anything but is best for quick activities that are completed more than once a week. When ready to post your feedback, you'll likely have numerous students who should receive the same comments. So, if 12 of my students mastered the activity, I write the entire SE2R feedback conversion, the content next to M in Figure 5.1, in one student's comment section. Now, much as a teacher in the grade world would do if these 12 students scored 20/20, I copy the complete SE2R feedback that has been added to one student's record and paste it into the remaining 11 students' comment boxes. For five students who wrote less than 300 words, I write the < 300 conversion (Figure 5.1) in one student's comment box. Again, I copy it and paste it into the other four comment areas for those students who received the < 300 note on my clipboard. This process continues for all students, and it takes 10 minutes or less to post feedback for a class of 30 students. Best of all, rather than learning nothing from a number or letter grade, every student knows exactly what was accomplished and what, if anything, needs to be done to complete the task. Because I've already talked to each individual, some may choose to ignore the written feedback. Still, a record exists for other shareholders—parents, counselors, and other teachers.

Remember, a score of 14/20 says, "You're finished, and you got a C," and the student will likely shrug and think, *Who cares? I'm average.* Meanwhile, the SE2R conversion will invite this student to return to the activity and complete something that is missing, in order to demonstrate mastery learning. And the purportedly average student will do it every time, moving from average to expert, often in the same day.

Although shorthand SE2R simplifies the process of providing written feedback, it isn't always needed when discussing an activity with students individually. It's easy through summary and explanation to help the student see what should be added to demonstrate understanding. For example, in the novel reflection critique, if a vocabulary word were missing, a student would most likely go to the word bank at that very moment, locate a word that works in the critique and add it to the blog post. Sometimes, I would be on the other side of the classroom discussing another student's writing, and a student would invite me back to reassess the critique with the missing vocabulary word or something else from the activity guidelines.

> This is the power of involving students in this insightful dialogue about learning.

At that point, an entirely different conversation may take place. "Why did you choose this word? Were you considering others? Is it possible to use a different form of the word to improve the writing?" Even though a student may have needed one element to demonstrate understanding of a particular concept or skill, the student may continue to expand on the work when challenged with a few key questions. This is the power of involving students in this insightful dialogue about learning. Granted, every activity can't be handled this way, but when it can, mastery learning happens quickly, and this is a beautiful thing.

THE SE2R PORTFOLIO

As indicated throughout this book, the most important reason to eliminate grades is that they take the student out of the assessment process. A feedback system provides a narrative that leads to a fascinating conversation with students about learning, which makes all forms of measurement obsolete. When teachers provide written feedback throughout a school year, this narrative can be collected and maintained in one place, creating an SE2R portfolio.

Teachers have been using portfolio assessment for many years. This involves placing various work samples that students have created throughout a school year and housing them in large folders or boxes. The theory is that students, parents and, perhaps, students' future teachers can evaluate the work to see how individuals have progressed over time. Portfolio assessment is well intentioned, but the problem is that the folders and boxes of work too often remain in a closet collecting dust, or they are sent home with students never to be used again. Even if these compendiums of work are reviewed, it's difficult to see authentic achievement, as activities are covered in number and letter grades, obscuring the net worth of the work— what was learned.

If Sarah has a pile of essays with scores ranging from 22/25 to 80/100, what does she learn from this? There's no consistency in how activities are valued, so even if the percentages are used to measure achievement, this too is meaningless. Sarah scores 88% on one writing sample (22/25). Later in the year, she manages only 80% (80/100). Did her writing competency decline? Using these indiscriminate numbers and percentages, it's impossible to know. However, if Sarah's work samples contain SE2R feedback, the portfolio's value increases exponentially. Still, the box of papers and projects can be discarded and replaced with a digital representation of Sarah's work, containing only the feedback she's received and how she has resolved it.

The SE2R portfolio is a large sample of feedback a student has received throughout the school year (Figure 5.2). The portfolio should be created when the first SE2R is given. It's worthwhile to give up an entire class period to teach students how to effectively create and manage the SE2R portfolio because it will ultimately represent the most valuable picture of their academic growth—far superior to a final report card and a GPA. If possible, the SE2R portfolio should be created and maintained in an online space; a cloud-based file is best. Examples include a classroom website, blog page, Google Doc, or Dropbox file. Teach students to create categories for the different kinds of work they'll create throughout the year. An elementary grade math teacher might ask students to generate these categories: *Math Facts, Word Problems, Projects, Lab Activities.* Note the *Resolution* column in Figure 5.2; this is the portfolio's most vital section, because it's where students will write how they resolved any part of an activity or project that was unfinished. This is how redirection is handled.

Each time feedback is provided, students record the feedback in the proper category in their SE2R portfolio. This is easy for narratives that students receive digitally (more on digital feedback in Chapter 6). For example, students could copy comments received on a blog post and then paste the feedback into their SE2R portfolios, maintained in a separate web page. As previously noted, pivotal to the success of the SE2R portfolio is that students write how they respond if redirection and request for resubmission were given; this is the *Resolution* section in Figure 5.2. This part of the process can't be overemphasized. Like having students evaluate themselves (more on this in the next section) and asking questions that elicit self-evaluation, the SE2R portfolio is critical to a student's growth as a self-evaluative independent learner. Being critical of one's own actions is a highly underrated life skill. If teachers begin cultivating this skill early, students will flourish not only in their K–12 lives but also in college and in their careers. SE2R portfolios should be updated weekly; again, this is extremely valuable class time.

Figure 5.2 SE2R Portfolio

My Feedback

PAGE [Edit · Files · Versions · New]

Date	Reflection Blog Posts	Book Chat	Feedback Resolution
9/2		You participated in a book chat with three peers in your group. You shared details about your book. You did not ask any questions about others' books. To improve listening skills, it's important to ask at least one question.	**September 13** I asked two people in my group questions about their books during this chat.
9/5	You completed a 250-word reflection letter on your blog. You clearly identify one key setting in your story. However, you didn't explain how the setting impacts decisions the characters make. Please add this explanation to your post. Let me know when you have done so.		**September 7** Last night I added two sentences to my blog. I said that Ponyboy was at the movies. He decided to go alone in a dangerous neighborhood. So he got jumped by the socs. Mr. Barnes said I accomplished the task.

Source: Barnesclass.com.

69

As the year progresses, updating the portfolio will take less time. Soon, students will begin discussing their entries with peers. Plus, each time they see feedback that redirects them, they'll want to return to activities, make changes and resubmit. Students become eager to add to the resolution section of their portfolios, as they realize this demonstrates mastery, which stirs pride in learning. And this is the kind of pride that is worth encouraging.

TALKING ABOUT FEEDBACK

Supplying effective feedback requires far more than jotting down observations of student work. "As it happens, applying feedback in complex situations is challenging. A fairly daunting list of things can undermine its effectiveness. Feedback can be too vague to be actionable. It can be specific and clear only to have recipients misunderstand it" (Lemov, Woolway, & Yezzi, 2012, p. 108). Avoiding these issues, while not easy, can be done through conversation with students. As noted in several places throughout this book, conversation about learning is an invaluable part of the SE2R process. However, up to this point, not much has been written about discussing the feedback that students receive. The primary motivation behind discussions about feedback should be to clarify any misunderstanding of it and to help students make the feedback actionable. According to *Practice Perfect* authors, Doug Lemov, Erica Woolway, and Katie Yezzi (2012), experienced educators, "Recipients may signal that they take feedback seriously, that they value it, but this does not necessarily mean that they use feedback" (p. 109). There is nothing complex about conversing with individuals about feedback. However, it is part of a successful no-grades classroom that teachers often neglect. This is understandable. Teachers are accustomed to observing student activities and responding, typically with opinion. Once they become skilled providers of SE2R, it's easy to be swept away by the thrill of summarizing,

explaining, redirecting, and request-
ing resubmission. Then, students
start responding to the feedback,
and the excitement swells because
this kind of reaction from students is
uncommon in the grades world.

> Tell students that the
> process of self-evaluation
> is as important as anything
> they will ever do in a
> classroom.

When I became overly engaged
in writing feedback, I told myself to slow down and talk about
the feedback with my students. This reminded me that conversations about feedback are as important, possibly more so,
than the original SE2R. These conversations encourage young
learners to become self-advocates, which is the primary goal
in a student-centered classroom. "Once students have bought
into the idea of self-advocacy (even if still reluctant to take the
first step), it's time to get them reflecting. Reflection is a tremendous tool, where students can really think about a specific
assignment and their journey through it" (Sackstein, 2014). A
perfect time to slow down and reflect on learning is when
students are reviewing feedback or adding it to their SE2R
portfolios. Here is a list of questions that can be used as a
starting ground for successful conversations that bring students into the assessment process, helping them become self-
advocates:

- What is your reaction to this?
- What will you do next?
- Do you agree with my explanation of what you did?
- What have you learned that you didn't know before
  the activity?
- What could you have done differently to improve?
- What prior lesson, model, or guideline did you revisit
  for help?
- Did you spend time reviewing the work and reflecting
  before you submitted it?
- How are your resolutions looking?
- Why didn't you resolve this activity/project?
- Are you satisfied with this?

Modeling this conversation in advance will help students visualize what can otherwise be an embarrassing conference, especially with shy students who are uncomfortable talking to teachers. Remember, most students will have never participated in a discussion about how they respond to teacher feedback. Tell students that the process of self-evaluation is as important as anything they will ever do in a classroom. Remind them constantly that their opinions about how they learn are the opinions that matter most. This ongoing process is what leads to self-advocacy.

REPORT CARD TIME: NOW WHAT?

When discussing SE2R feedback in place of grades at schools and conferences, it doesn't take long for a teacher or administrator to ask about report cards. "I can eliminate grades during the marking period, but I still have to put a grade on report cards," is a common complaint. Many years ago, when I decided to stop grading, I knew the report card would pose a problem. This is an issue that must be confronted early in the school year with all stakeholders—students, parents, and administrators. When explaining the no-grades system to students in August, they always ask about report cards. This is one of my favorite parts of the year, because of their reaction to my response. "We'll discuss your progress over the course of the marking period," I explain, "and we'll decide on the grade together." Lots of puzzled looks follow. Talking about grades makes sense; most students have done it in the past with teachers who ask them what they believe their grade should be and to justify their opinions. Even in these cases, the teacher always makes the final judgment, typically based on how the math adds up. There were 1,000 points possible. Paul amassed a total of 710, good for 70% and a report card grade of C. Any discussion about this is nothing more than smoke and mirrors. Familiar with this ruse, students persist: "Okay, but you're still going to tell us our final grade, right?" This is where the jaws really drop. I inform them that we'll reflect on their accomplishments and discuss how their work fits in the A, B, C's of the grade world but, in the end, they will decide the final grade. Students never really believe this until the end of the marking period arrives and we discuss the grade and decide on it.

In order to effectively discuss and decide on a final report card grade, it's necessary to set aside several days for individual conversations. The first year I conducted grade conferences, I tried to squeeze them into two days. My average class size was 25. I assumed each conference would take no more than three minutes. This was a huge miscalculation. The average grade conference took five minutes and some took 10. Three or four days was necessary to complete effective conferences, as these turned into awe-inspiring discussions about learning over time. It's easy to assume this is impossible, with other objectives that must be met in a marking period, but this is some of the most useful time you'll spend with students all year.

Photo from thinkstockphotos.com.

Student decides her report card grade.

In preparation for the individual grade conference, I ask students to review all of their work from the prior grading period. They look at everything they've done online, visiting their web pages, blogs, and most important, their SE2R portfolios. During conferences, students are busy reviewing everything and considering how this fits into the letter grade matrix. We have abandoned grades, but they've been graded their entire school lives so they understand the basics. Also, we talk about this prior to the conference, and I emphasize that I don't want to reduce their learning to A's, B's, and C's.

There have been times when I said nothing at all about how students should determine their report card grades. "You know how grades work. Consider what you've accomplished and figure it out." After five minutes of reviewing activities and feedback, most easily settled on a letter that I would then place on the report card. Other times, I've had groups that were less confident in their abilities to examine a large amount of schoolwork, voluminous narrative feedback, and to conclude what their report card grades should be. This is understandable; it's a unique challenge to return to the constraints of the grades world once you're accustomed to residing in a world where learning is centered on conversation and self-evaluation. So, we discussed guidelines for deciding on a final report card grade. We agreed that a marking period filled with completed activities and mastery, based on resolution of all redirection to prior learning, merits a report card grade in the A to B range. Although few, if any students, receive D's or F's because they've been given the chance to rework activities, we agree that if 60 percent or less of our work was not revisited and resubmitted, this would equate to a grade in the D to F range.

> Grade conferences turn into goal-setting sessions.

Individual grade conferences turn into so much more than labeling work with a letter. As students discuss their accomplishments and the learning outcomes they believe they didn't master in a grading period, their self-evaluation skills begin to grow. "I'm writing more than ever," a student would say, "but I still need to cut down on my mechanical errors." In effect, grade conferences turn into goal-setting sessions. This, of course, fans the intrinsic motivation that encourages students to work harder moving forward. I've experienced students who struggled to adjust to the no-grade system and failed to resolve the SE2R they received on numerous activities and projects. When it's time to put a grade on a report card, and students give themselves a D or an F, it means much more than a teacher doing it, especially when the students have to tell their parents that they decided on the low mark. Imagine a parent asking, "Why did your teacher give you an F?" and the response being, "He didn't give me an F. I gave it to myself." The parent–child conversation that follows is one more important part of the feedback continuum.

PERFORMANCE REVIEW

Like the one-room schoolhouse, corporal punishment, and note taking on slates, report cards will one day disappear from schools worldwide. Some visionary school administrators like those at Anastasis Academy in Colorado solved the problem by never using report cards in the first place. Anastasis founder Kelly Tenkely (2014) did not want assessment based on data. "In starting Anastasis Academy, we quickly found that no traditional grading system could adequately assess students as they were learning. We ditched formal A to F grading and instead used standards-based grading. The idea was that if we assessed students based on standards (which we used as some of our learning goals), stakeholders would be able to better map progress as they went."

What troubles educators and policy makers, who lack the vision to eliminate measurement, is how to demonstrate learning at the end of a school year. How can students be promoted to the next level and, eventually, to college without a report card? There are many methods of demonstrating learning without letters and GPAs. Since education is rapidly moving into the digital world, work samples can be maintained in the cloud. Over the course of one school year, activities and feedback can be deposited into an online folder, similar to an SE2R portfolio. This sort of digital portfolio assessment is still in its infancy, but it is not new. Big Picture, a large consortium of progressive schools that embrace student-centered learning, use digital portfolios in lieu of grades as a means of introducing students to college admissions deans. "Such assessments authenticate for the student what she knows and validates for the teacher what the student knows and how she knows what she knows—not only the student's know-what but know-how and even know-why" (Big Picture Learning, 2014). In fact, teachers, school counselors, and college admissions deans can easily access academic growth from the years of content that students curate in digital files. Students can carry this library of achievement with them on mobile devices. Imagine having the ability to sit down with a teacher or college professor and quickly respond to any request for a work sample with the swipe of finger.

> It is amazing what happens when you take away the labels and help kids understand that no matter where they start from, there is something to be learned, forward progress to be made. They choose lofty goals. They do the impossible.
>
> —Kelly Tenkely, co-founder, Anastasis Academy

A valuable part of this digital compilation of student work and feedback should be performance reviews. A performance review is similar to what teachers receive when evaluated by administrators. It is a narrative about one's abilities, skills, knowledge base, and growth over time. This is a part of narrative feedback that often elicits a knee-jerk reaction of, "There's no time for that." Like the report card conference and individual conversations about learning, the performance review is a critical piece of student growth. It is similar to a report card in only one way—the best way. The intention of a report card is to summarize learning; as noted throughout this book, it fails miserably. The performance review also summarizes learning, but because it is a written report by a teacher or team of teachers who have spent a school year assessing student accomplishments and discussing those accomplishments with each individual, the performance review succeeds where the traditional report card fails. Plus, performance reviews can be used as part of the college admission process. "How does a student get into college without a GPA?" people ask. The answer is a large digital portfolio and years of meaningful written assessments from teachers and the self-evaluations of students.

There are many ways a teacher can create performance reviews that simplify the process. One such method is to involve as many teachers as possible. This is easy if the document is created in a cloud-based file. In the sample team performance review on page 78, a page is created in a Google Doc for reviews of Laura Johnson, a fictitious student. Mr. Fox, the language arts teacher, adds his review, and the document will be shared with Laura's other teachers, and they can enter the document at their leisure and post their reviews. This approach is especially easy in elementary schools, where students have fewer teachers, and in schools that use academic teaming. If multiple teachers have the same group of students, the entire roster can be divided equally. Each teacher will create the performance review documents for a segment of students, lightening the workload for all. For example, on a team of 120 students, four teachers might each set up 30 documents. One teacher should coordinate the effort, creating a folder that contains all student reviews and sharing it with others. It takes two to four weeks to complete this many reviews, depending on how much is written on average per student, so the process should begin with roughly one month of school remaining.

Writing performance reviews for 100 or even 50 students may seem like a daunting task, but each one may vary in length and doesn't have to be too long. The review Mr. Fox writes is just over 200 words. It might take five minutes to accomplish this task, so the time it takes to complete performance reviews

Performance Review for Laura Johnson 2013–14 school year

Mr. Fox (language arts): You completed two year-long projects and demonstrated exceptional growth in many skills through these projects. In the beginning of the year, you were a reluctant reader and admitted you'd never read a book voluntarily. During our Reading All Year Project, you selected and read 17 books, a remarkable accomplishment that deserves to be celebrated. While reading these books, you completed weekly reflections in which you discussed characters and plot and made many comparisons to other experiences and life lessons, based on what you read. You also completed our diary-writing project; you posted more than 70 entries (an average of two per week). Your character took life through your writing, and you eliminated many of the mechanical errors you were making at the beginning of the year. Specifically, you have mastered basic sentence structure, no longer writing run-ons or sentence fragments. You show expertise in the basics of comma use and capitalization. You have good command of vocabulary. You presented numerous oral presentations with clarity and good voice. You collaborate well and easily evaluate your own learning. You've shown excellent growth throughout the year and have much to be proud of. You discovered books this year. Please continue reading, and everything else will be easy.

Miss Wade (science):

Mrs. Rogan (social studies):

Mr. Kosar (math):

Mr. Sanchez (Spanish):

for all students could total as little as five or six hours. Breaking this task up over time, though, will lessen the burden, and *burden* is really an inaccurate term, because reflecting on all students' growth and sharing your observations with them is a truly rewarding experience. If you make assessment an ongoing conversation throughout the year, you might be uncomfortable writing a performance review, without each student's voice. In this case, you might share some or all of your performance review with your students and invite them to add their own reflections about the school year. I was always astonished by the honesty of students about their own learning. "It still sounds like a lot of work," people have told me. Of course it's work. There's not much about being a teacher that isn't. The end result though is magical. "It is amazing what happens when you take away the labels and help kids understand that no matter where they start from, there is something to be learned, forward progress to be made. They choose lofty goals. They do the impossible" (Tenkely, 2014).

REFLECTION

Brainstorm some SE2R shorthand that you might use on a future assignment. Consider reviewing Figure 5.1 as a guide. Convert the shorthand into complete SE2R feedback. How much time will shorthand SE2R save?

In an effort to involve students in the feedback process, consider creating a focus group of students who can help you write SE2R and create shorthand notes. What feedback does the focus group provide that helps facilitate a conversation about learning in your class?

Feedback in a Digital World

Technology is nothing. What's important is that you have a faith in people, that they're basically good and smart, and if you give them tools, they'll do wonderful things with them.

—Steve Jobs, American entrepreneur and inventor

It was April of 2007. Presidential primary debates were beginning. Even if the major TV networks didn't cover them live, most were available via streaming Internet feeds. A unit on persuasion was next up for the English language arts class, and this seemed like a perfect opportunity to meet students on their favorite playground—the Internet. An online message board was created, and students were instructed on its use. I invited them to view a Democratic Party debate from South Carolina State University on an Internet newsfeed. While watching the debate online, students were to post comments and questions to the message board.

> I didn't realize it at that moment, but the message board gave birth to digital feedback in our class and initiated what would later become Assessment 3.0.

That night, I sat at my old desktop computer scrutinizing the performances of eight presidential hopefuls, including eventual two-term president Barack Obama. The candidates' rhetoric, however, was far less exciting than the activity on our new classroom message board. Only about four minutes passed before the first comment was posted. Soon another student joined, followed by a third and a fourth. Ten minutes later, there were 18 eager participants. Their comments and questions were awkward at first (this was, after all, new ground for these teenagers). They posted opinions on Hillary Clinton's hair, Joe Biden's tie, and Mike Gravel's age. Eventually, though, the cafeteria-style discussion turned serious. "He didn't answer the question," one student wrote. "Right," another chimed in, "he was asked about the war in Iraq, and he spent the whole time talking about a woman in New Hampshire." I smiled inwardly as this web-based conversation continued. I posted a couple of questions and responded to several comments, and the message board discussion raged on throughout the 90-minute debate.

The next day, students burst into the classroom chatting about how much fun it was discussing the debate on the Internet. They hungered for similar assignments and requested other message board activities. Students wanted to communicate about learning online, which was amazing considering the circumstances. It was late in the school year, when the only thing most students care about were their upcoming vacations. Had I asked them to watch the debate in class on a television and write about it in a notebook, the activity would have likely been a colossal failure. Given the opportunity, however, to interact with each other using a nonconfrontational platform, my students couldn't get enough. I didn't realize it at that moment, but the message board gave birth to digital feedback in our class and initiated what would later become Assessment 3.0.

GIVING STUDENTS WHAT THEY WANT

During the summer of 2007, I spent many hours searching for a web-based platform that would broaden student engagement. The message board was only a doorway to an amazing world of online learning. One all-inclusive classroom website could change everything. So, I searched for something that included a message board, a place for lessons and work samples, and most important, individual student web pages. Eventually, the quest ended at the wiki host, EditMe, and led to the creation of our new one-stop-shop for learning—Barnesclass.com, pictured in Figure 6.1. The goal

Figure 6.1 Feedback in the Digital World

of the classroom website is to give 21st-century digital learners an interactive hub, where they can communicate with the
teacher, parents, and peers. This learning management system, or LMS, is like a digital backpack. It houses activity
guidelines, video instruction, projects, conversation, and it is
a place for both public and private narrative feedback.

It took a couple of years before I understood the diversity
of the classroom website; using it as a feedback tool eluded me
at first. In the beginning, it was a vibrant playground for
learning. Students uploaded video and graphic presentations
and wrote daily journals and other lengthier prose, all to demonstrate understanding of concepts and skills. Prior to the
advent of the Results Only Learning Environment and SE2R
(Summarize, Explain, Redirect, Resubmit), I would review
students' work on Barnesclass.com and put a number or letter
grade on it, as I had done for so many years. It wasn't until my
research on motivation, collaboration, and feedback that the
site's role expanded, and it became an invaluable assessment
tool. Students have access to the classroom website from anywhere with an Internet connection, and when updates are
made, the teacher gets an email alert that includes a direct link
to the student's web page. This virtual world made it easy for
me to leave feedback from anywhere and with any Internet-
ready device, including a smartphone.

Feedback Tools That Engage Learners

It wasn't long before students' attitudes about our classroom
site cooled. With new websites and applications cropping up
daily, a teenager's fascination with web tools ebbs and flows.
We continued to use the classroom website throughout the
school year for a variety of teaching and learning activities,
but for writing and posting pictures, graphics, and media,
students wanted something different. Enter the classroom
blog, which filled many of the same roles that the website did,
with one major exception. The blog is a social network that

encouraged students to share their work and comment on what peers were doing. As student interest and my understanding of the blog and other web tools increased, so did the use of an assortment of digital resources. Accompanying this online activity was SE2R feedback and, best of all, independent learning.

The Blog

The modular nature of the wiki-hosted classroom website makes adding features like a message board, page menu, and embeddable slide shows easy. For a time, the website was an all-inclusive digital classroom. The site even included its own blog, which sufficed for writing and sharing for a brief time, but as stand-alone blogs improved over time, the blog on our classroom website became obsolete, and we needed something else. Following another summer of research, I settled on Kidblog, which is designed by teachers for teachers. Kidblog (Figure 6.2) created a different kind of learning management system—one that added the social networking features that students covet. Once it was linked to Barnesclass.com, students could easily navigate to the classroom Kidblog host site and to their individual blogs. It wasn't long before daily journals, book reflections, and persuasive essays populated each student's blog, all grouped by class in alphabetical order, so they could be easily located by their peers and by teachers. Students enjoy posting articles and other media on blogs. Not only is the blog a digital book, it is a portfolio of activity that an individual can share with peers, adults, and depending on how it's administered, the world. Blogs invite conversation, which leads to feedback. "When students feel as though the space belongs to them, there is a sense of ownership in what is posted. There is also a freedom that comes with having your own 'web site' where you can talk about the things that matter to you the most" (Utecht, 2010).

Students responded beautifully to feedback on their blogs. In addition to posting articles daily on their own niche subjects (a critical component to successful classroom

Figure 6.2   Class Blog Containing Video Instruction

Source: Kidblog.org.

blogging), students wrote about class discussions, books, online articles, and videos. More important, they reflected on their own learning. Their posts provided a wonderful platform for SE2R feedback. Some class days, students wrote for most of the period. Sitting in the middle of the room as they worked, I watched their writing come to life and zealously typed feedback into the comment section beneath their articles. "Hey, Lauren," I would shout across the room, interrupting the rhythmic taps echoing from 25 computer keypads. "Refresh your page; I just left feedback for you." When Lauren reloaded her blog post, she found detailed SE2R comments beneath her prose (Figure 6.3). Sometimes, within minutes, Lauren might reply, "Mr. Barnes, I read your feedback and made changes. Can you check my post again?" I can't remember a time in the many years I spent placing low scores on a student's writing that she would make immediate changes and ask me to reassess her work. It just doesn't happen in the world that attempts to measure learning with numbers and letters, and this is the most egregious part of traditional grading. Recall what Coppell East's Laura Melson noticed: Narrative feedback that redirects students, as the SE2R in Figure 6.3 does, and invites them to resubmit activities for further review inspires students to demonstrate mastery and show off their skills. I would argue that no student wants to show off work after receiving a 60/100 or a D.

Figure 6.3 SE2R Blog Entry

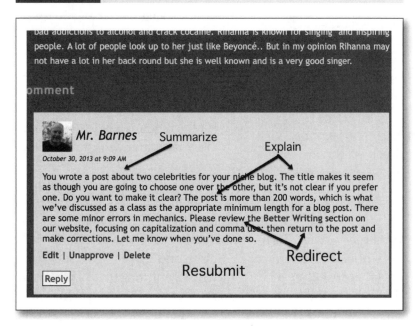

Social Networks

"A math teacher halts a lecture, projects incomplete math theorems on the board, and then assigns a different problem to each of several small groups. The twist is that the students post a photo of their written progress to Instagram every 90 seconds so that the instructor can monitor responses in real time" (Alfonzo, 2014). It would be difficult to find a better example of formative assessment using social media than this. Social networks create powerful technology toolkits, with which teachers can provide and acquire the kind of immediate feedback that fuels the conversations and problem-solving processes that are critical to learning. Twitter has been used at the college level for years, and teachers in K–12 classrooms are quickly seeing its value as a formative assessment tool for all ages. In 2013, two European college professors experimented with Twitter and made several noteworthy conclusions. Chief among them was that Twitter created a unique conversation that encouraged reciprocity and shifted instruction from a "reliance on formal structures to the growth of social media as a learning space" (Rich & Miah, 2013).

> I made time for the students to review their initial work and redo the areas where they were struggling, based on the dialogue that we had in the Google document.
>
> —Hadley Ferguson, teacher and education author

Teachers worldwide are beginning to understand the simplicity of the social media learning space that Emma Rich and Andy Miah describe, especially when it comes to formative assessment and narrative feedback. Kathy Cassidy, author of *Connected From the Start: Global Learning in the Primary Grades,* assesses her first graders through Twitter discussions (2013). Author and International education presenter Shelly Terrell (2014) suggests a variety of social networks for student collaboration and teacher and peer feedback because this is how students want to learn. "They crave feedback in the form of likes, retweets, mentions, reblogs, and tags. The trend is to be more social and participatory and the web is evolving swiftly with new technologies, apps, tools, and trends to enhance these experiences. It's time we tapped into the potential of these developments to engage our students in meaningful collaboration, research, and writing."

Consider how Hadley Ferguson constructed a no-grades classroom, built on conversation and collaboration. Ferguson (2013) highlights the importance of an ongoing dialogue with students about what they're learning.

> I used Google Docs to comment on every piece of work and to encourage the next steps. I read all of their work and then left them comments, identifying the areas of strength and pointing them toward ways to improve on what they had done. . . . I made time for the students to review their initial work and redo the areas where they were struggling, based on the dialogue that we had in the Google document. I wanted the students to see that reviewing and rethinking past work was important, that each assignment served a purpose. (p. 198)

Ferguson's approach sounds a lot like SE2R feedback, with the emphasis being on the two R's (redirect and resubmit), where real learning takes place. Google Drive's social component makes this piece easy and it instills a sense of autonomy in students.

Mobile Devices and Applications

As Shelly Terrell suggests, students enjoy sharing on social media. What they may love even more is using mobile devices. "About three in four (74%) teens ages 12–17 say they access the Internet on cell phones, tablets, and other mobile devices at least occasionally" (Maden, Linhart, Duggan, Cortesi, & Gasser, 2013, p. 1). The fact that students have a world of learning at their fingertips and teachers often ignore it is unfathomable. Not only does mobile learning uncover limitless possibilities for lessons and activities, it puts narrative feedback in our students' hands. There are hundreds of applications that make providing feedback easy. My students used many of these throughout the school year. They read books and posted summaries and reviews to the social network Goodreads using the site's mobile

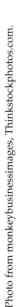

Putting feedback in students' hands.

application. I accessed Goodreads from my iPhone, iPad, or desktop computer to easily supply feedback about their writing.

When I wanted instant feedback from students about a recent skill or concept we had studied, I turned to the text messaging app, Celly, which offers a private texting room that hides all phone numbers and gives the administrator the ability to moderate any or all messages. Celly allowed me to quickly see what students had or had not mastered on a given activity, based on their responses to a few simple questions. From there, if I needed to supply more detailed feedback that I didn't want their peers to see, I could go to our private message board on our class website or simply pull them aside for an individual conversation. Students love their devices, so they will always read feedback and respond as long as teacher comments are meaningful. Had I texted, "You failed this activity," the student would certainly have spurned the use of Celly in the future, seeing it as just another punitive grading tool.

CONTENT CURATION AND FEEDBACK

Although it is a relatively unknown phrase in education, *content curation* is one of the most underrated and indispensable

21st-century skills. "We are obligated to teach our students how the information that they curate may ultimately define them and may impact innumerable people in their society" (Barnes, 2014, p. 12). The first person content curation impacts is the student because this content becomes a critical part of two-way feedback and self-evaluation, which is a primary ingredient in the no-grades classroom. When using a social network like Goodreads or Diigo, a social bookmarking site, students curate their own libraries. They add books to shelves marked *read* and *to read* and create links to websites, which house important class-related information and research. They annotate and review content and interact with teachers and peers, both in class and from around the world. The knowledge students provide and the skills they demonstrate on social networks like these are invaluable. In essence, content curation on social media creates an ongoing digital conversation about learning. Teachers and peers can supply insightful feedback to the curators, which helps them add to or change their ever-growing libraries of information. More important, students become highly critical of their own work because they come to realize that they are building vast repositories for not just classmates or teachers, but for the world. The decision-making process behind the kind of content that is shared involves reflection and metacognition, necessary life skills that are not always taught in school.

Consider your own curation habits. If you have a Facebook page (a likely non sequitur since well over a billion people do), you are a content curator. That is, you locate or create information and you share it with various audiences. In most cases, you consider numerous variables that help you decide whether to post this content. Sure, some of these decisions take seconds. Not much consideration prefaces the "Just landed in Boston; so glad to be home" post. However, when it comes to news or entertainment that is unrelated to your personal life, you think more deeply about what you share, especially if the content is relevant to your profession. An *Edutopia* article about mobile learning may land in your email inbox. You find it worthy of sharing on your Facebook, Twitter, or

Pinterest page. Will you simply share the link or will you annotate what you share, analyzing it and adding your opinion? Regardless of what you decide, this is that important reflective process mentioned earlier. Some people add news links with simple comments like, "You may find this interesting," while others criticize what they're sharing with remarks such as "This would never work in Finland." Consider how often you scroll through your social media pages, reviewing what you've shared. Aren't there times when you regret something you published or the comment you made about it? You wonder what motivated you to share it; in some cases, you might even delete it, hoping no one has viewed it. This is the metacognitive process that many content curators ignore but a process that plays an integral role in responsible content curation.

There is much to be learned from this kind of self-evaluation, and teaching this to students is a responsibility that is more important now than it's ever been. "Talking about thinking is important because students need a thinking vocabulary. During planning and problem-solving situations, teachers should think aloud so that students can follow demonstrated thinking processes. Modeling and discussion develop the vocabulary students need for thinking and talking about their own thinking" (Blakey & Spence, 2008, p. 1). In addition to helping students understand how to think about the decisions they make about learning, in general, we must encourage them to consider the choices they make on social media. Not only do teachers have to help their students understand the remarkable impact they have on the world when it comes to content curation, we also need to recognize the precious opportunity to use social networks and content curation to create and maintain insightful conversations about learning. The digital tools empower teachers to begin the conversation. It's as easy as commenting on what students are sharing. Questions like "Why did you post this?" or "Did you consider how this comment impacts your peers' opinions about it?" spark reflection and metacognition while helping to initiate the two-way feedback process. Imagine the impact of inviting students to assess their own content curation using SE2R. It's unfathomable how a teacher could even think about putting a grade on this activity. I do believe, however, that the engagement and learning would be immense.

REFLECTION

- How do you decide what to share on social media? How do your students decide?
- Can you use social media for assessment in your classroom?
- What barriers exist with using social media for class activities and for assessment?

Discuss this with all education shareholders at your school. Remember to emphasize the value of technology for learning and feedback, while recognizing the equal importance of appropriate use.

Tips for Success

A successful man is one who can lay a firm foundation with the bricks others have thrown at him.

—David Brinkley, journalist

As I sat waiting for students to arrive for a new school year, I was stricken with fear of the change I was about to make in my teaching. Gone were the workbooks, worksheets, and lecture notes that helped me through each class period. Brief instructional videos, collaboration, and digital learning would replace them. As if planning for a chaotic learning environment wasn't enough to increase my anxiety, I had to figure out a way to fix our online grade book so it wouldn't show failing grades for my students. I scrolled from one screen to the next, searching for an answer to a problem no one had ever encountered; everyone in my school graded assignments with numbers and, based on those numbers, the online program calculated a percentage and a letter grade. If I left an assignment with no numerical value, the program defaulted to a grade of 0.0%, F. This certainly wouldn't sit well with parents.

A colleague entered my room. She asked what I was doing and I explained. After some surprise at my declaration about eliminating grades, she began a more detailed inquiry. "How will students react? What about your special needs kids? Many of them don't do well with change. What will counselors and administrators say? What about parents?" During my time contemplating my own problems transitioning to a results-only classroom, I hadn't fully considered these issues. While troubleshooting the online grade book and worrying about student-centered lessons, I neglected to think about parents, administrators, counselors, and my entire student population. I needed answers to a lot of questions, and I needed them before my students arrived in less than 20 hours.

A PROACTIVE APPROACH

I spent an hour with my colleague that day, engaged in a helpful dialogue about the issues she'd raised. We even worked through my online grade book problem so that it stopped giving students zeroes and F's for missing assignments. I spent a lot of time that first year making mistakes and figuring things out as the school year passed. The lessons I learned about reshaping how one teaches and, especially, eliminating grades were critical to creating a successful no-grades classroom. Most important was the understanding that a proactive approach is necessary when changes impact students and parents and catch the attention of administrators. Replacing grades with SE2R feedback is a tremendous change that few parents understand and most administrators fear. Rather than waiting to react to questions and ultimatums, it's best to tackle these issues from the beginning. The following sections outline various ways to be proactive in creating a no-grades classroom.

Explain How It Works to Students

After that critical hour-long discussion years ago, I decided to introduce the Results Only Learning Environment (ROLE) to my students on the first day of school. Pushing aside the textbook and syllabus, I created a slide show that would help me explain what would be a whole new world of learning for my students. As mentioned earlier, I told them I would never put a number or letter grade on anything they produced in class. They discussed this briefly before I fielded questions about it.

Depending on when you read this book, for it may not be at the beginning of the year when you delve into narrative feedback, it's still important to take considerable time in class and explain how the system works. Here is a list of areas to cover in the discussion:

- Explain the value of feedback over grades (for older students share research).
- Introduce SE2R or another feedback system you may be using.
- Show examples of feedback.
- Invite students to talk about it and to ask questions.
- Discuss the ramifications of redirection (deadlines typically disappear).
- Underscore the importance of resolving problems when redirected.
- Discuss self-evaluation.
- Explain how the feedback process leads to mastery learning.
- Explain how report cards are handled.

Talk to Administrators

We were five weeks into the school year before my principal knew I had stopped grading my students. When she asked why there were no letter grades on our midquarter progress reports, I informed her that I was no longer grading any activities or projects, so giving students a letter grade on an interim report would only mislead parents. Instead, I had left a single comment for all students that said, "Satisfactory progress." This was certainly not an effective report in a class built on detailed, descriptive feedback, but our grade program had a limited library of comments, and this one worked best at the time. Fortunately, the principal at my school was a progressive-minded educator, and she was intrigued by the new no-grades approach. We talked more about narrative feedback and SE2R, and I explained how final report cards would be handled. Other administrators and guidance counselors were less open to the no-grades classroom, and because I waited until problems cropped up to discuss the issue, it was difficult, if impossible, to convince some of them of the value of narrative feedback.

This is why it's so important to be proactive and discuss a no-grades classroom with all principals, counselors, and other teachers as soon as the change is implemented. If possible, use the same approach outlined in the previous section; in other words, explain feedback over grades, much as you do with students. Many educators have never considered no-grades assessment and have little understanding of how it works. A few years ago, I taught on an academic team. About a week before the school year started, we all met at my home to create team policies and to discuss consistent classroom practices. This meeting served as the perfect opportunity for me to broach my SE2R system and invite colleagues to adopt a similar method of assessment. They weren't ready to make the giant leap to a no-grades classroom but they understood my methods, which was important since we had the same students and accessed the same online grade book. Creating a comfort level with colleagues and administrators is the first step to a smooth transition. Be sure to open a dialogue about why you choose the no-grades classroom and how objective narrative feedback and two-way conversations about learning benefit students. Emphasize the goal of creating self-evaluative independent learners. The conversation about learning makes this easy, while attempting to measure learning inhibits independent mastery of concepts and skills. It's not important at this point that administrators agree to transition to a no-grades system. The key to the conversation is encouraging them to consider the value of SE2R and ongoing dialogue about learning. As the year progresses, you can invite them to see the impact of the no-grades classroom on your students. In time, they will understand this and a conversation about systemwide change may ensue.

A LETTER TO PARENTS

"As long as parents understand, I'm fine with it." This is what the principal said, when I told her about involving students in final report card grades. Suddenly, the anxiety I had felt that August day, when I was deciding how to handle my first class as a results-only learning teacher, returned. One quarter into the school year, my students' parents knew only what their children had told them about our class, and 12-year-olds aren't extremely forthcoming when it comes to sharing information at home. So, I wrote about our feedback system on the classroom website and explained how report cards would be treated, but only about 25 percent of the parents were using the website. Sure enough, when report cards went home, emails and phone calls poured in. Parents wanted to know why their children had a particular grade. They didn't understand it because the online grade book had no numbers or letters. In subsequent years, I decided it would best to be proactive and explain Assessment 3.0 in the beginning of the year. Here is one version of a letter to parents that examines the grading issue and explains how assessment functioned in our class.

Dear Parent:

I am excited about our upcoming year in language arts, and I have something very special to share about how learning will be assessed in our class. Your child will never receive a number or letter grade on any activity. Research indicates that measuring learning with numbers, percentages, and letters is an inadequate way to assess learning. Numbers and letters say very little about academic achievement.

Your child and I will evaluate learning together, using an ongoing dialogue. I will provide both written and verbal narrative feedback about what your child has accomplished and what may still need to be learned. You can review this feedback in the online portfolio we will create and in the comment section in the online grade book. The feedback approach to assessment leads to self-evaluation and ultimately to mastery learning.

Your child will spend ample time reviewing completed activities and what was learned and we will discuss how this fits into the A, B, C grade world that students and parents are accustomed to. After this evaluation and our discussion, your child will decide what the final report card grade should be. This process will help your child become a self-critical independent learner.

If you have questions, please email or call me. Thanks for your support.

The parent letter paves the way to further understanding of the feedback system and leads to useful conversation about assessment and mastery learning as the school year progresses.

Continue the Conversation

After a few years of using SE2R in lieu of grades, I received the most challenging group of students I'd had in 20 years as a classroom teacher. This group contained students with severe needs, students who were repeating seventh grade, and students with emotional issues. A large percentage of the 115 students were considered to be at risk of failure. These were not people who adjusted well to change. Many of these students fought the no-grades system, which was a rare occurrence. In fact, only a handful of students had ever complained about the system up to that point, and most loved receiving SE2R feedback and the opportunity to discuss report card grades.

> We embraced the mantra: "Production, Feedback, Change."

This challenging group of students, though, many of whom had failed in school most of their lives, struggled with being given the opportunity to resolve issues with their class work. When a reluctant learner wrote a sentence on a blog post, instead of a 300-word analysis or reflection, I explained that I needed to see lengthier writing so I could have a clear picture of strengths and weaknesses. In the beginning of the year, some reluctant learners would sigh heavily and say things like, "Can't you just give me an F?" These students exemplify exactly what is wrong with the current grade system. When students are conditioned to fail, they see no value in learning; thus, even when faced with engaging assignments that will enhance skills that are necessary in school and in life, they believe they can't succeed.

At first, I was confounded by students who didn't want to resolve the problems in their work. Prior to that year, if I instructed students to write more, they would simply say "OK," and happily return to their writing. Most of those students had a different approach to learning, though, for one reason or another. The key to reaching the students who initially recoiled from SE2R feedback was to simply talk more about it. Returning to my Day-One slides, I spent a class day reminding students about the value of feedback. We talked about self-evaluation and how students' opinions of their own work were more important than a teacher's opinion. We discussed autonomy and intrinsic motivation. I explained that students would be given plenty of choices and that everything they did would have a purpose. They were reminded that a simple mark on their work would be less valuable than feedback and that they should relish the opportunity to improve their work because it gives them a chance to demonstrate how much they know. We embraced the mantra "Production, Feedback, Change." This mantra, I emphasized, was the key to obtaining that goal of mastery. About one-third of the way into that difficult school year, students stopped asking for grades, and they began resolving issues with activities and projects.

Assessment 3.0 relies heavily on constant discussion of the value of narrative feedback and the path to mastery learning that it creates. Not only do students have to be reminded, but parents do, too. The communication lines must remain open, and feedback and self-assessment should be at the forefront of all conversations. At open houses and parent-teacher conferences, I always kept material on hand about feedback. There are many articles available online about the deleterious effects of grades and the impact of narrative feedback. Stacks of these sat on chairs outside my room, where parents waited for their conferences to begin. While I could answer most questions about our system, it was helpful to have a source other than me to share with parents, reassuring them that narrative feedback isn't some bizarre lab experiment that one rogue teacher created.

Administrators and colleagues should be included in the ongoing conversation about the elimination of grades and the influence of SE2R. During three or four days of report card grade conferences, I shared many examples of the astonishing things students said about learning with my colleagues and my principals. These brief chats would always spark follow-up questions that helped remove fears of something that was largely unknown to most. Plus, the more I could inspire administrators to reflect about feedback, the bigger the possibility that they would consider encouraging other teachers to use it. So, remember, talk to all stakeholders about Assessment 3.0. Like anything, the more conversation there is about it, the more comfortable people will be with it.

CELEBRATE INDEPENDENT LEARNING

Educators love to celebrate. We cheer our athletic groups, our orchestras, and the debate team. When our children climb rock walls at school picnics, teachers shout, "Hooray!" Unfortunately, we also celebrate grades. Kindergartners receive stars for coloring inside the lines, and third-graders' perfect spelling tests are lined with smiley faces. When students are old enough for GPAs to be calculated, the ones with report cards littered with A's and B's are placed on honor and merit rolls. Some schools conduct elaborate ceremonies for these extra special students, where ribbons and ovations are lavished upon them generously. Meanwhile "bad" students, who were unable to manipulate the system well enough for the "good" grades, watch in envy or disgust. Enough has been written in this book that I don't have to offer detailed information on the negatives related to celebrating grades. This section is about celebrating the kind of learning that accompanies narrative feedback and the independent learners that evolve in a no-grades classroom.

While teachers in results-only classrooms will never cheer perfect scores or high grades, it is important to emphasize the epic accomplishments of students who learn to appreciate the value of teacher feedback and their own self-evaluations. Not only is it okay to pat students on the back when they review SE2R comments, return to prior learning, and revise something so they can master it, this type of celebration is necessary. As the Coppell East teachers note in Chapter 4, students who have lived in the traditional grades community for so long sometimes struggle with the adjustment to classes built on feedback and self-assessment. Some resist openly, asking for points to be placed on their projects and activities. They are used to working for a mark, and many are accustomed to being praised by educators and parents for "good" grades and extrinsic rewards. When students transition to a feedback assessment model and become proficient self-advocates, this is something truly worth celebrating. So, pat them on the back. Celebrate your entire class and be sure to remind them of precisely what they have accomplished. At various times throughout the school year, I stood in front of my class and proudly announced to students, "You have become insightful, self-critical learners—the very best kind of learner there is. Let's cheer for ourselves and for each other." The response to this celebration is far more rewarding than any ceremony that culminates with a medal being draped around a student's neck.

EVALUATE YOUR APPROACH

In an effective Assessment 3.0 system, we encourage students to self-evaluate. The more critical you are on yourself, we tell them, the more successful you will be. Still, no matter how much we harangue our students to self-assess, we often fall short when it comes to evaluating our own work. When you write feedback weekly, assessing your own work is crucial to the success of the no-grades classroom. In Chapter 3, I admitted how I unwittingly allowed subjectivity to make its way into my SE2R. Once I began reading the feedback I had written as if I were the student it was intended for, it became clear that much of it didn't fit my own SE2R model. This process of reviewing the SE2R I was writing for students helped me produce more effective feedback in the future.

In addition to assessing written feedback, you should also consider how you're presenting lessons and how you write activity guidelines. As noted earlier, writing clear, detailed activity and project guidelines makes providing meaningful feedback easy. When explaining to students something that was not accomplished, this explanation must clearly match the instructions, or confusion can arise. Recall the teachers from Coppell East. They used a collaborative self-evaluation model to monitor their success, as they transitioned from traditional to results-only classrooms. "The three of us met weekly during content time to touch base," Kat Julian says.

"Those weekly check-ins were very helpful in keeping us motivated and accountable and just to debrief what was working and what needed to change." According to Julian, East principal Laura Springer gave the pilot team one day every six weeks for self-evaluation and planning. "We had a whole day to go over our plans, align ROLE structures across grade levels and, most importantly, go over our feedback to learners and to each other. We would discuss how successful or unsuccessful our feedback strategies and documentation were going, as they were evolving over the year. Discussing each other's feedback styles and our transformations was by far the most beneficial part of the transition."

Just as students' skills and activities evolve over the course of a school year, based on meaningful narrative feedback, teachers in a student-centered class, built on Assessment 3.0, evolve as they evaluate their own methods, strategies and the feedback they supply. Using a collaborative approach like the one employed by the Coppell East pilot team is certainly one that all teachers should emulate.

REFLECTION

Consider how you might create a no-grades culture in your classroom. Ask colleagues and administrators to combine efforts in making a plan for using SE2R feedback at your school. Like the pilot team at Coppell East, rely on this accountability group to help you take a proactive approach to change. As a team, brainstorm ideas for making a smooth transition away from traditional grades. Work together on one step to smooth the transition—like composing a letter to parents about your no-grades classroom and your feedback model.

Conclusion

*When something is important enough, you do it even if
the odds are not in your favor.*

—Elon Musk, businessman

Ninety-three years after the first presidential election ended in 1779, Susan B. Anthony, arguably the world's most popular suffragette, became the first woman to vote outside of the Wyoming territories in a formal election. She was subsequently arrested and convicted for breaking the law that precluded women from voting. In 1920, more than 14 decades after Anthony's bold move and that first presidential election, Congress passed the Nineteenth Amendment to the Constitution, and women were finally permitted to vote. Sadly, America's most famous female voter died 14 years before this historic event. Without the extraordinary efforts of Susan B. Anthony and other suffragettes, who battled oppression for centuries, it's conceivable that women might still be waiting for the right to vote. While it may seem like a far-fetched analogy, I believe that the no-grades classroom is, as voting once was to the suffragettes, an unrealized dream that is in desperate need of its own champions.

A Grassroots Movement

Susan B. Anthony and lesser-known leaders of their own women's rights movements like New Zealand's Kate Sheppard and Ireland's Louie Bennett were instrumental in helping women gain the right to vote in their respective countries.

> When a few teachers make major changes in their classrooms and share them openly with their colleagues, administrators, and surrounding schools, the roots begin to grow and spread.

Because women around the world at the time were subservient to men, even the suggestion that they should be able to vote was rebuffed swiftly, sometimes violently, by their male counterparts and local lawmakers. To achieve their dream, Anthony and the others were forced to start small. So, they recruited other women from their hometowns. They distributed flyers summarizing their goal. They quietly organized groups to spread the word and combat the laws that oppressed them. As they grew in number, their voices became louder. They started gathering publicly and they demonstrated at major events. The suffragettes' grassroots programs eventually turned into regional and ultimately national movements and powerful women's unions that could no longer be overlooked by politicians.

While I would never compare the issues confronting educators to the tyranny that women have faced, and I certainly hope it doesn't take 14 decades for assessment to change, I do believe that teachers should follow a path like the one paved by Anthony, Sheppard, and Bennett. Educators can write books and blogs and speak at conferences, but the quickest way to eliminate traditional grades and to begin a conversation about learning in schools is to start our own grassroots movements. As the teachers at Coppell East Middle School demonstrate, when a few teachers make major changes in their classrooms and share them openly with their colleagues, administrators, and surrounding schools, the roots begin to grow and spread.

TIME FOR A REVOLUTION

James Pillans' blackboard and chalk changed how teachers shared information, and it's time for a similar renovation. When it comes to assessment, the ineffectiveness of numbers and letters is irrefutable. Like women gaining the right to vote, eliminating grades is an inevitable revolution and an idea whose time has come. Teachers worldwide are already implementing systems built on narrative feedback; they are creating grassroots movements that are spreading across schools, districts, cities, and states. The Internet is chock-full of articles and videos about progressive education and involving students in conversations about learning. More colleges are accepting students without traditional grades, accentuating the use of digital portfolios and teacher recommendations. Students in classrooms built on narrative feedback routinely outperform their traditionally graded peers on standardized tests, quashing any argument that students can't pass tests without a consistent record of grades on worksheets and other practice activities.

There was a time when it was inconceivable that students could produce schoolwork on anything other than a small piece of slate. Then the spiral notebook was invented, making the slate obsolete. If I had written a book 10 years ago, suggesting that notebooks, like the 19th-century slate, would soon disappear and be replaced by thin electronic tablet computers, I might have been branded a heretic. Yet, now schools across the world use tablets every day. Like the teachers who have replaced pencil and paper with tablet computers, we need to remain open to the possibility of other bold initiatives like the no-grades classroom if education is to continue to evolve.

THE FUTURE IS NOW

Fast forward to the year 2050. You enter a school where grade levels no longer exist; instead, students advance based on their own skill levels. A 10-year-old boy learns calculus, and a

16-year-old girl spends most of her day studying music and art because she has had all of the core subjects that she desires. There are no bells, and students traverse hallways at random intervals because traditional class periods disappeared long ago. There is no attendance office because students arrive at different times throughout the day, based on when classes meet or when they need to see a teacher. There is no assistant principal in charge of discipline; school is an engaging environment, where students focus only on the joys of learning. You walk by several rooms and see teachers involved in deep conversation with individual students, while other students rest comfortably on cushioned chairs or sofas, reviewing written feedback, making changes to activities, while waiting for a turn to converse with the teacher. There is no measuring of learning. No numbers on papers and no letters on report cards. Of course, this doesn't surprise you. Seeing grades would be as archaic as those ancient spiral notebooks and pencils. How teachers ever measured learning with numbers and percentages is incomprehensible.

Now, rewind to the current year. That school of the future may not seem so futuristic. There are many schools without bells, using alternative schedules. Not so long ago, my own school adopted a system in which students moved about at different intervals, and teachers dismissed them by checking the time and announcing that class had ended. Some schools teach students based on their knowledge; it's not uncommon in those places to see sixth graders taking ninth-grade courses. And, as noted in numerous places throughout this book, many teachers assess learning with narrative feedback and conversation with students about what they've accomplished.

For these teachers, grades are like slate and chalk, like paper and pencil. These educators have looked to the future and seen schools without grades. They have witnessed the remarkable power of narrative feedback, conversation about learning, and student self-evaluation. They have known students to become amazing, critical, independent learners. They have seen the brilliance of a classroom without judgment, completely bereft of any subjectivity. They've experienced a future classroom, built on Assessment 3.0, and they have decided that the future is now.

Appendix A

Feedback From the Field

W hen I was completing research for this book, I reached out to many educators and other education share-holders from many places, asking for feedback about their experiences with Assessment 3.0. The response was so over-whelming that there was no way for me to integrate every-thing into the narrative. Teachers, parents, and administrators supplied their own takes on SE2R and a no-grades classroom, and some provided amazing quotes from students, who are part of no-grades classrooms. This is a compilation of comments from these remarkable people—all trying to change the world.

SE2R allows me to develop and enhance the working rela-tionship I have with each student. Rather than worrying about the grade, students know that they can persistently wrestle with concepts and skills, and that I will provide them with the necessary guidance until they feel comfort-able with what we are learning, without the fear that their GPA will suffer. This is not to say that students choose A's for themselves; far from it, actually. Several students who have earned acceptances to the Ivy League and other top-tier universities have assigned themselves C's and D's at various points in the term because they felt they had not yet mastered our coursework. I suspect that this level of self-awareness and honesty, especially amongst teenagers when it comes to grades, may only result because we have chosen to focus on learning in our classroom as opposed to letter and percentage-based grades.

—Charles Gleek, teacher, Broward Prep Academy

I feel like the feedback I have received so far has been extremely helpful. The feedback always makes me feel like I'm doing a good job, but also gives me insight as to how I can improve my writing.

—Sophia, 11th grader, Broward Prep Academy

One practice I have learned over the years is to not expect perfection on the first try. I've been in the teaching field for more than 25 years at this point, and I still have a great deal to learn, so how can I expect undergrads, average ages between 19 and 22, to know how to teach a small group of six-year-olds? How could I expect perfect timing and unity in style of an undergrad student's interaction with children's spontaneity in a short lesson, and then for the student to write that up for me to be read with clarity and style? What scoring grade should be placed on that work? I never give letter or number grades to these assignments. Instead, we have a conference together with verbal conversation and suggestions on what was terrific and what could be changed on the next lesson with the undergrad and the children.

—Dr. Stacy Reeves, professor,
University of Southern Mississippi

I really enjoy seeing the comments on my work. It's much better than receiving back an essay or homework assignment where there is just a 9/10 on the top and not knowing where I went wrong. I am grateful for all teachers who take the time to leave feedback on all of their students' work, and I understand that it can often take a long time to do so.

—Isabella, 11th grader, Broward Prep Academy

When teachers stop grading, they can really begin to help their students where they need help. Take for example two students in the same English class. One writes an essay with interesting ideas and technical problems, the other a technically perfect essay but with no original ideas. In the traditional grading system, the student with the technically perfect essay will undoubtedly fare better, even though she needs to be encouraged to take risks with her ideas. The other student, who would probably get a low grade, needs to be encouraged to work on her technical skills while maintaining her voice and ideas. Once grades are abolished, both students can work on their own weaknesses without fear of failing.

—Sara Bennett, coauthor of The Case Against Homework

I feel that an emphasis on summative assessment, especially with younger students, creates an environment where learning ends, and that is not the environment I want for my students. Students learn and understand skills and concepts at different rates. I do not believe in using assessment in a punitive manner, essentially punishing students for what they do not understand. We use the word *yet* often in reflecting upon our own learning. At the same time, we are looking to help students own their learning and progress. Progress is essential, and we want our kids to be able to assess themselves in their forward movement.

—Michelle Baldwin, teacher, Anastasis Academy

Grading is a math exercise. Ten items. Three with answers that don't match the answer sheet. Each item worth ten points. 3 × 10 = 30. 100–30 = 70. Math problem. The teacher has shown you she can do simple math. Remember, this teacher has shown you she can grade; she hasn't shown you she can assess.

—Kylene Beers, author and former
president of the National Council of Teachers of English

I was very pleased with the feedback that I received. While writing my responses, I was overcome with the feeling that I was much less worldly than I had previously thought—that I wasn't as aware of conflicts around the world as some of my classmates. However, your feedback made me feel encouraged and intelligent. You pointed out what I should be working on, but you managed to do it in a nice way while also praising what I did correctly.

—Josie, 11th grader, Broward Prep Academy

My students self-assess using the SE2R method. They identify which parts of the standard they have cogently addressed, as well as areas that can be further developed. At times self-assessment is written, but other times it is done via a conversation with me. These conversations are very one sided with the student taking the lead in explaining their thoughts about their work. Narrative descriptive feedback has changed the culture of my learning environment. Students are engaged in the learning process and not just working for a grade. There is no more point seeking behavior, and learning is the goal for my students. Narrative feedback gives my students direction in their learning. It reinforces areas of strength while providing opportunities for growth and improvement. Grades don't enhance the learning experience, but feedback does.

—Garnett Hillman, Spanish teacher, Lockport Township High School

I think that the feedback that I have received has been very helpful in the fact that it allows me to see what I can really improve upon. My feedback has helped me to understand what I need to refine and hone in on. I think that getting feedback is much more helpful than just getting a grade. Instead of doing an assignment, getting a grade and moving on, I find myself really thinking about ways to fix my work.

—*Jordan, 11th grader, Broward Prep Academy*

The fear of what grade she made was taken away and she could learn without the fear of failure.

—*Susan Hall, parent of a child in a no-grades classroom*

I think that the feedback is a system that will help me a lot in the future. The feedback I receive is very helpful when I'm on target, and even more helpful with helping get back on target if I'm off. The best thing, I think, about feedback is that it gives me the opportunity to correct myself without worrying about a bad grade. It lets me take a shot at the answer, even if I'm not sure I'm right, because I know that the worst that can happen is I improve through critique.

—*Miranda, 11th grader, Broward Prep Academy*

To hear fifth-grade students take control of their learning, to own up to where they should have worked harder, to set up their future path for learning—wow. This is what assessment should be.

—*Pernille Ripp (2014, p. 117)*

When grades are removed (which requires a huge cultural shift, I realize) and the focus is on doing quality work, the students begin to develop habits of deeper learning and thinking, not because they are motivated by a grade but because they are socially accountable for their best work. (Socially accountable in terms of how tasks should be amplified so that work is shared with a global audience for feedback.)

—*Mike Fisher, education author and researcher*

I have been able to tell students what they are doing— what I notice, at the very least. Sometimes they don't see it themselves. This can be very powerful for students, and I get to know them much better in the process. Letting them know the effect it has on me is another step in the process.

—Joy Kirr, teacher, Arlington Heights SD25

Appendix B

SE2R Feedback Quick-Reference Guide

I t took years of honing SE2R feedback, before I believed what I was writing was truly effective. I'm not sure any of it was perfect, because writing objective, descriptive feedback with proper redirection is a complex, constantly changing process. The toughest challenge is helping students fully comprehend feedback and how to use it. The strategy that best helped students was encouraging them to use SE2R on their peers and on themselves. If students use the same SE2R model that teachers use, they become highly critical of their own work, and the quality of their assignments and projects will improve. These SE2R models are designed to serve as guides for teachers and students in all grades. Feel free to print and distribute these models to all education shareholders.

SE2R Feedback Model for Teachers

Summarize: Provide a one- or two-sentence summary of what students have accomplished on an activity or project.

Explain: Share detailed observations of what skills or concepts have been mastered based on the specific activity guidelines.

Redirect: Instruct for students the lessons, presentations, or models that need to be reviewed in order to achieve understanding of concepts and mastery of skills.

Resubmit: Encourage students to revisit activities or projects after redirection, rework them, and resubmit for more feedback.

SE2R Self-Check for Students Grades 4–12

Summarize: Do I understand what I have accomplished on the activity or project?

Explain: Do I know which skills or concepts I learned or did not learn based on the specific activity guidelines provided by my teacher?

Revisit: Which lessons, presentations, or models do I need to review in order to achieve mastery learning? Do I need extra help? What should I do again to show that I've learned?

Resubmit: Am I ready to give the changed activity or project back to my teacher for more feedback?

SE2R Self-Check for Pre-K–3

Summarize: Do I know what I did?

Explain: Did I learn all the things my teacher taught me?

Redo: What should I try again because I still don't know it? Should I ask my teacher for help?

Resubmit: Am I ready to give my work back to my teacher so it can be checked again?

Appendix C

SE2R Feedback You Can Use Today

SE2R Examples for any Subject or Grade

Summarize

You completed a (name project type here) that demonstrates your understanding of the laws of physics as discussed in class.

You created a bio poem that fits the class model.

You wrote a 500-word essay on the pros and cons of making Patriot Day a national holiday.

You ran one mile without stopping.

You drew a picture that illustrates your knowledge of horizon line in perspective drawing.

You completed various parts of a debate based on lessons and class models of formal debate.

You conjugated five Spanish verbs per the guidelines presented in class.

SE2R Examples for any Subject or Grade

Explain

You show understanding of (concept title here) in numbers in most of the assigned problems, but you have not demonstrated understanding on number X. What happened here?

Your essay is the appropriate length and contains proper capitalization based on our lessons. You provide two arguments on the pro side but only one on the con side. Can you supply another example of a con in your argument?

Effectively using the horizon line to guide your drawing, you drew a car, similar to the one modeled in class. The specifications of your car meet all project guidelines.

You met the first goal of running an entire mile without stopping. Your time of 8:41 is 41 seconds off of your goal. Should you adjust your goal?

SE2R Examples for any Subject or Grade

Redirect

Revisit the (lesson type) and review the (concept name). Then, complete problem X correctly.

Review the two articles you found about national holidays. Locate one more fact or opinion that supports the con side of your argument and add it to your essay.

Consider the five steps to successful distance running that we learned in class. Evaluate your last attempt at an eight-minute mile. Practice the steps that will help you improve your time. Or, let's discuss a new goal for your next attempt.

Review the video on our class website about the rise and fall of the Mayan society. Locate two details from the video that give evidence of the rise and fall of the Mayans. If you struggle to locate these details, see me for help. When you find them, add them to your written response.

SE2R Examples for any Subject or Grade

Resubmit

Show me problem X when you have corrected it.

When you've added the con side of the argument to your essay, post a message telling me you've done so on our class message board.

When you are ready to run the mile again, ask a classmate or friend to time you and tell me your time or tweet it to me, using our class Twitter handle.

When you rework problem X on your activity sheet, give it back to me so I can check it again.

Arrange a time to present your new project ideas to me after class or send them to me via email.

References

Alfonzo, P. (2014, May 20). *Frictionless formative assessment with social media*. Retrieved from http://www.edutopia.org/blog/friction less-formative-assessment-social-media-paige-alfonzo

Barnes, M. (2011, July). Isn't it time to eliminate grades in education? [Online forum comment]. Retrieved from http://www.ted .com/conversations/4478/isn_t_it_time_to_eliminate_gra.html

Barnes, M. (2013). *Role reversal: Achieving uncommonly excellent results in the student-centered classroom*. Alexandria, VA: ASCD.

Barnes, M. (2014). *Teaching the iStudent: A quick guide to using mobile devices and social media in the K–12 classroom*. Thousand Oaks, CA: Corwin.

Big Picture Learning. (2014). *Performance assessment: Assessing know-how as well as know-what*. Providence, RI: Author. Retrieved from http://www.bigpicture.org/2008/11/performance-assessment-assessing-know-how-as-well-as-know-what/

Black, P., Harrison, C., Lee, C., Marshall, B., & Wiliam, D. (2004). Working inside the black box: Assessment for learning in the classroom. *Phi Delta Kappan, 86*(1), 9–21.

Blakey, E., & Spence, S. (2008, December 16). *Developing metacognition*. Retrieved from http://www.education.com/reference/article/ Ref_Dev_Metacognition/

Bower, J. (2013). Reduced to numbers: From concealing to revealing learning. In J. Bower & P. L. Thomas (Eds.), *De-testing de-grading schools: Authentic alternatives to accountability and standardization* (pp. 154–168). New York, NY: Peter Lang.

Butler, R., & Nisan, M. (1986). Effects of no feedback, task-related comments, and grades on intrinsic motivation and performance. *Journal of Educational Psychology, 78*, 210–216.

Cassidy, K. (2013). *Connected from the start: Global learning in the primary grades.* Virginia Beach, VA: Powerful Learning Press.

Coley, R. J. (2000). *The American community college turns 100: A look at its students, programs, and prospects.* Retrieved from http://www.ets.org/Media/Research/pdf/PICCC.pdf

Concordia Online Education. (2012). History of the classroom blackboard. Seward, Nebraska: Author. Retrieved from http://education.cu-portland.edu/blog/reference-material/the-history-of-the-classroom-blackboard/

Ferguson, H. (2013). Journey into ungrading. In J. Bower & P. L. Thomas (Eds.), *De-testing de-grading schools: Authentic alternatives to accountability and standardization* (pp. 194–209). New York: Peter Lang.

Guskey, T. (2011). Five obstacles to grading reform. *Educational Leadership, 69*(3), 16–21.

Harris-Perry, M. (2012, April 19). Let's get rid of grades. *The Washington Post.* Retrieved from http://www.washingtonpost.com/opinions/lets-get-rid-of-grades/2012/04/19/gIQAwie5TT_story.html

Hattie, J., & Timperly, H. (2007). The power of feedback. *Review of Educational Research, 77*(1), 81–112.

History of the classroom blackboard [Web log message]. Retrieved from http://education.cu-portland.edu/blog/reference-material/the-history-of-the-classroom-blackboard/

Johnson, L. (2014). High marks for no marks. *Wellesley Magazine, 6.* Retrieved from http://www.wellesley.edu/sites/default/files/assets/departments/admission/pdf/shadowgrading-cuba.pdf

Kohn, A. (1999, March 1). *From degrading to de-grading.* Retrieved from http://www.alfiekohn.org/teaching/fdtd-g.htm

Kohn, A. (2011). The case against grades. *Educational Leadership, 69*(3), 28–33.

Lemov, D., Woolway, E., & Yezzi, K. (2012). *Practice perfect: 42 rules for getting better at getting better.* San Francisco, CA: Jossey-Bass.

Maden, M., Linhart, A., Duggan, M., Cortesi, S., & Gasser, U. (2013, March 13). *Teens and technology 2013.* Retrieved from http://www.pewinternet.org/2013/03/13/teens-and-technology-2013/

Marklein, M. (2013, February 13). Grades pointless? Some colleges don't care about GPAs. *USA Today.* Retrieved from http://www.usatoday.com/story/news/nation/2013/02/27/college-grade-point-averages/1947415/

Pink, D. (2009). *Drive: The surprising truth about what motivates us.* New York, NY: Riverhead Books.

Rich, E., & Miah, A. (2013, March 13). Can twitter open up a new space for learning, teaching and thinking? *The Guardian.* Retrieved from http://www.theguardian.com/higher-education-network/blog/2013/mar/13/twitter-transform-learning-higher-education

Ripp, P. (2014). *Passionate learners: Giving our classrooms back to our students.* Virginia Beach, VA: Powerful Learning Press.

Sackstein, S. (2014, February 12*). Letting go of the reins to allow for student self-advocacy* [Web log post]. Retrieved from http://starrsackstein.com/category/letting-go-of-the-reins-to-allow-for-student-self-advocacy-originally-ran-on-finding-common-ground-on-12312013/

Tenkely, K. (2014, July 10). *We choose the moon: Assessment without labels* [Web log message]. Retrieved from http://ilearntechnology.com/?p=5346

Terrell, S. (2014, January 15). *Fostering meaningful peer collaboration with digital tools* [Web log message]. Retrieved from http://shellyterrell.com/2014/01/15/feedback/

Thomsen, M. H. (2013, May 1). *The case against grades: They lower self-esteem, discourage creativity, and reinforce the class divide.* Retrieved from http://www.slate.com/articles/double_x/doublex/2013/05/the_case_against_grades_they_lower_self_esteem_discourage_creativity_and.html

Tomlinson, C., & Moon, T. (2013). *Assessment and student success in a differentiated classroom.* Alexandria, VA: ASCD.

Utecht, J. (2010). *Blogs as web-based portfolios.* Retrieved from http://www.thethinkingstick.com/images/2010/06/Blogs-as-Web-Based-Portfolios.pdf

Wiggins, G. (2012, September). Seven keys to effective feedback. *Educational Leadership, 70*(1), 10–16. Retrieved from http://www.ascd.org/publications/educational-leadership/sept12/v0170/num01/Seven-Keys-to-Effective-Feedback.aspx

Wiliam, D. (2011). *Embedded formative assessment.* Bloomington, IN: Solution Tree Press.

Winne, P. H., & Butler, D. L. (1994). Student cognition in learning from teaching. In T. Husen & T. Postlewaite (Eds.), *International encyclopedia of education* (2nd ed., pp. 5738–5745). Oxford, UK: Pergamon.

Index

ABC evaluation approach, 8
Advanced Placement (AP)
     courses, 40
Alfonzo, P., 88
Anastasis Academy (Colorado),
     75, 113
Ancillary evaluation items, 29–30
Anthony, Susan B., 107–108
Arbitrariness, 14–15, 22–24, 29–30
Assessment 2.0
     arbitrariness, 14–15, 22–24, 29–30
     background, 7–9
     community college effect, 17–18
     failure mentality, 9–10, 19–20
     grade–learning connection, 9–12,
          18–20
     grade point averages (GPAs),
          8, 15–16
     student involvement, 59–61
     subjectivity, 12–14, 22–24
Assessment 3.0
     accountability, 6
     barriers, 5–6
     communication lines, 102
     future directions, 108–110
     grading practices, 4–5
     impact, 95–96
     proactive action plans, 96–100
     user feedback, 111–116
     see also SE2R (Summarize,
          Explain, Redirect,
          Resubmit)
Aungst, Gerald, 29–30
Authentic feedback, 32–33

Baldwin, Michelle, 113
Barnesclass.com, 83 (figure), 83–84
Barnes, M., 6, 18, 45–46, 91, 118,
     119–122
Beers, Kylene, 113
Bennett, Louie, 108
Bennett, Sara, 113
Big Picture Learning, 76
Blackboards, 1
Black, P., 19
Blakey, E., 92
Blogs, 62–64, 84–87, 86 (figure),
     87 (figure)
Bower, J., 10
Boyd, Megan, 46, 47–49, 56
Brinkley, David, 95
Brock, Jim, 16
Broward Prep Academy (Florida),
     40–43, 112, 115
Butler, D. L., 125
Butler, R., 19

Cassidy, K., 88
Celly, 90
Christina (case study), 47–49
Classroom blogs, 84–87, 86 (figure),
     87 (figure)
Classroom websites, 83 (figure),
     83–84
Cloud technology, 68, 76, 77
Coley, R. J., 17
College admission requirements,
     15–16
Community college effect, 17–18

Concordia Online Education, 1
Conferences, grade, 72–75
Content curation, 90–93
Coppell Middle School East
  assessment practices, 21, 45–46
  Christina (case study), 47–49
  evaluation practices, 104–105
  feedback process, 52,
    53–54 (figure), 55
  pilot team, 46
  success rate, 55–58
  Tori (case study), 49–52
  transition challenges, 46–47
Cortesi, S., 89
Cuba, Lee, 16

DeRanek, Carissa, 41–42
Digital feedback, 81–90,
  83 (figure)
Digital portfolios, 76
Diigo, 91
Dropbox, 68
Duggan, M., 89

EditMe, 83

Facebook, 91
Failure mentality, 9–10, 19–20,
  100–102
Feedback
  authentic feedback, 32–33
  challenges, 70–72
  classroom blogs, 84–87,
    86 (figure), 87 (figure)
  content curation, 90–93
  Coppell Middle School East case
    study, 45–58, 53–54 (figure),
    104–105
  digital feedback, 81–90,
    83 (figure)
  grade–learning connection,
    18–20, 55–58, 60–61, 100–104
  importance, 31–32
  narrative feedback, 31–33
  SE2R portfolio, 67–70,
    69 (figure), 76
  SE2R shorthand strategy, 62–66,
    63 (figure)

student involvement, 59–79,
  81–83
  see also SE2R (Summarize,
    Explain, Redirect, Resubmit)
Ferguson, H., 46–47, 55, 88, 89
Fisher, M., 12, 115
Franklin, Benjamin, 59

Gasser, U., 89
Gladwell, M., 45
Gleek, Charles, 40–43, 111–112
Goodreads, 89–90, 91
Google Docs, 52, 68, 77, 89
Google Drive, 89
Grade conferences, 72–75
Grade–learning connection, 18–20,
  55–58, 60–61, 100–104
Grade point average (GPA),
  8, 15–16
Grading practices
  ABC evaluation approach, 8
  arbitrariness, 14–15, 22–24, 29–30
  Assessment 2.0, 7–12
  background, 2–6, 7–9
  community college effect, 17–18
  failure mentality, 9–10, 19–20,
    100–102
  grade–learning connection, 9–12,
    18–20, 55–58, 60–61, 100–104
  grade point averages (GPAs),
    8, 15–16
  grassroots movements,
    108–109
  report cards, 72–75
  self-grading assessments, 42–43
  subjectivity, 12–14, 22–24
  see also SE2R (Summarize,
    Explain, Redirect, Resubmit)
Grassroots movements, 108
Guskey, T., 8, 32

Hadjas, Laurence Emmanuelle,
  17–18
Hall, Susan, 49, 50, 51–52, 115
Harrison, C., 19
  see also Black, P.
Harris-Perry, M., 8–9
Hattie, J., 19–20, 32, 36

Hillman, Garnett, 114
History of the classroom
   blackboard, 124

Independent learners, 55, 103–104
   see also SE2R (Summarize,
   Explain, Redirect, Resubmit)
Instagram, 88
International Baccalaureate (IB)
   courses, 40
Internet message boards, 81–82

Jobs, Steve, 81
Johnson, L., 16
Julian, Kat, 46, 52, 53–54 (figure),
   56, 104–105

Kidblog, 85, 86 (figure)
Kirr, Joy, 116
Kohn, A., 9, 32, 36

Labels, subjective, 12–14
Lao Tzu, 1
Learning–grade connection, 18–20,
   55–58, 60–61, 100–104
Learning management systems
   (LMSs), 83 (figure), 83–84
Lee, C., 19
   see also Black, P.
Lemov, D., 70
Linhart, A., 89

Maden, M., 89
Marklein, M., 15–16
Marshall, B., 19
   see also Black, P.
Melson, Laura, 46, 47, 49–51, 56, 87
Message board discussions, 81–82
Miah, A., 88
Mitra, Sugata, 7
Mobile devices, 89–90
Moon, T., 3, 19
Motivation, 9–10, 19–20
Musk, Elon, 107

Narrative feedback, 31–33, 61–62
   see also SE2R (Summarize,
   Explain, Redirect, Resubmit)

Next page is, 7
Nineteenth Amendment (U.S.
   Constitution), 107
Nisan, M., 19
No-grades assessment system,
   18–22, 40, 55–56, 89
   see also SE2R (Summarize,
   Explain, Redirect, Resubmit)

Performance reviews, 75–79
Pillans, James, 1, 109
Pink, D., 9, 13
Pinterest, 92
Portfolio assessment, 67–70,
   69 (figure), 76, 77, 109
   see also Blogs
Prezi Project, 24–28, 25 (figure)
Proactive action plans, 96–100
Punitive grading, 12, 24, 28–29, 37,
   48, 50, 90, 113

Reeves, Stacy, 15, 16, 112
Reluctant learners, 9–12, 100–102
Report cards, 72–75
Results Only Learning
   Environment (ROLE), 3, 45–46,
   49–50, 55–56, 58, 97
Rich, E., 88
Ripp, P., 60, 61, 115
Roberts, Greg, 16
Romanoff, John, 24, 26
Rubrics, 25 (figure)

Sackstein, S., 71
Sanders, Barry, 21
SE2R (Summarize, Explain,
   Redirect, Resubmit)
   administrative support,
      97–99, 102
   background, 32–34
   challenging students, 100–102
   classroom blogs, 84–87,
      86 (figure), 87 (figure)
   communication lines, 102
   Coppell Middle School East case
      study, 45–58, 53–54 (figure)
   evaluation practices, 104–105
   feedback challenges, 70–72

feedback examples, 119–122
grade conferences, 72–75
high school applications, 40–43
parental support, 99–100, 102
performance reviews, 75–79
proactive action plans, 96–100
purpose, 4
quick reference guide,
    117–118
sample assignment, 34–39,
    38 (figure)
SE2R portfolio, 67–70,
    69 (figure), 76
SE2R shorthand strategy, 62–66,
    63 (figure)
student involvement, 59–79
user feedback, 111–116
written feedback, 61–62
Self-advocacy, 71–72
Self-evaluation
advantages, 21, 110
assessment practices, 40
Christina (case study), 48
content curation, 91–93
grade conferences, 74–75
importance, 72, 101
portfolio assessments, 68, 77
SE2R (Summarize, Explain,
    Redirect, Resubmit),
    104–105
Self-grading assessments,
    42–43
Self-reflection, 71
Shadow grading, 16
Sheppard, Kate, 108
Shorthand SE2R strategy, 62–66,
    63 (figure)
Social networks, 87–89
Spence, S., 92
Springer, Laura, 45–46, 49, 56,
    57–58, 105
Standardized tests, 4, 6, 55–57
    see also SE2R (Summarize,
        Explain, Redirect, Resubmit)

Student involvement, 59–79,
    81–83
Subjective labels, 12–14
Success criteria, 95–100
Suffragettes, 107–108
Summarize, Explain, Redirect,
    Resubmit (SE2R)
    see SE2R (Summarize, Explain,
        Redirect, Resubmit)
Swarthmore, 16

TED Talks, 18–20
Tenkely, K., 75, 76, 79
Terrell, S., 88, 89
Text messages, 90
Thomsen, M. H., 8, 12
Timperly, H., 19–20, 36
Tomlinson, C., 3, 19
Tori (case study), 49–52
Traditional grading practices, 2–4
Twitter, 40, 88, 91

University of Southern
    Mississippi, 16
University of Virginia, 16
Utecht, J., 85

Websites, classroom, 83 (figure),
    83–84
Weighted assessments, 14–15,
    26–29
Wellesley, 16
White, E. B., 31
Wiggins, G., 32, 33, 36
Wiki-hosted classroom websites,
    83 (figure), 83–84
Wiliam, D., 19, 32
    see also Black, P.
Winne, P. H., 125
Women's suffrage, 107–108
Woolway, E., 70
Written feedback, 61–62

Yezzi, K., 70

A SAGE Company

Corwin is committed to improving education for all learners by publishing books and other professional development resources for those serving the field of PreK–12 education. By providing practical, hands-on materials, Corwin continues to carry out the promise of its motto: **"Helping Educators Do Their Work Better."**